SLAVERY AND ABOLITION
IN PENNSYLVANIA

In the Pennsylvania Historical Association's

Pennsylvania History Series,

edited by ALLEN DIETERICH-WARD AND DAVID WITWER

RECENT TITLES IN THIS SERIES:

James E. Higgins, *The Health of the Commonwealth: A Brief History of Medicine, Public Health, and Disease in Pennsylvania*

Judith Ridner, *A Varied People: The Scots Irish of Early Pennsylvania*

Roger D. Simon, *Philadelphia: A Brief History,* revised and updated edition

Judith Ann Giesberg, *Keystone State in Crisis: The Civil War in Pennsylvania*

G. Terry Madonna, *Pivotal Pennsylvania: Presidential Politics from FDR to the Twenty-First Century*

Karen Guenther, *Sports in Pennsylvania*

Marion Winifred Roydhouse, *Women of Industry and Reform: Shaping the History of Pennsylvania, 1865–1940*

Daniel K. Richter, *Native Americans' Pennsylvania*

BEVERLY C. TOMEK

SLAVERY AND ABOLITION

IN PENNSYLVANIA

THE PENNSYLVANIA
HISTORICAL
ASSOCIATION

TEMPLE UNIVERSITY PRESS
Philadelphia | Rome | Tokyo

TEMPLE UNIVERSITY PRESS
Philadelphia, Pennsylvania 19122
tupress.temple.edu

Published by Temple University Press in partnership with
    The Pennsylvania Historical Association

Library of Congress Cataloging-in-Publication Data

Names: Tomek, Beverly C., author.
Title: Slavery and abolition in Pennsylvania / Beverly C. Tomek.
Other titles: Pennsylvania history studies.
Description: Philadelphia : Temple University Press in partnership with The
    Pennsylvania Historical Association, 2021. | Series: Pennsylvania
    History Series | Includes bibliographical references and index. |
    Summary: "A general introduction to the topic of slavery and abolition
    in Pennsylvania. Synthesizes works produced in that field from its
    beginning at the turn of the century to the present day"—Provided by
    publisher.
Identifiers: LCCN 2021009470 (print) | LCCN 2021009471 (ebook) | ISBN
    9781932304350 (paperback) | ISBN 9781932304831 (pdf)
Subjects: LCSH: Pennsylvania Society for Promoting the Abolition of
    Slavery—History. | Antislavery movements—Pennsylvania—History. |
    Slavery—Pennsylvania—History. | Abolitionists—Pennsylvania—History. |
    Slavery—Economic aspects—Pennsylvania—History. | Free African
    Americans—Pennsylvania—History. | African Americans—Legal status,
    laws, etc.—Pennsylvania—History.
Classification: LCC E445.P3 T66 2021 (print) | LCC E445.P3 (ebook) | DDC
    326/.809748—dc23
LC record available at https://lccn.loc.gov/2021009470
LC ebook record available at https://lccn.loc.gov/2021009471

This book is dedicated to my friends in the PHA,

especially Karen Guenther,

my fellow UH Cougar and partner in crime.

Thanks for all the tours of fun and interesting Pennsylvania attractions,

including the various Sonic Drive-Ins we stopped at over the years.

CONTENTS

EDITOR'S FOREWORD

ON BEHALF OF THE MEMBERS and officers of the Pennsylvania Historical Association (PHA), we are pleased to present the fourth book in the redesigned Pennsylvania History Series (PHS). As part of the PHA's mission to advocate and advance knowledge about the history and culture of Pennsylvania and the mid-Atlantic region, the PHS remains committed to providing timely, relevant, and high-quality scholarship in a compact and accessible form. Volumes in the series are produced by scholars engaged in the teaching of Pennsylvania history for use in the classroom and broader public history settings. As we recently passed the seventieth anniversary of our first publication in 1948, a new partnership was forged with Temple University Press that now provides the series with the expertise, resources, and support of a respected academic publisher.

Dr. Beverly Tomek's scholarship on antislavery movements, particularly African recolonization in Pennsylvania, premiered roughly a decade ago in an article in *Pennsylvania History: A Journal of Mid-Atlantic Studies*. She has also published articles on slavery and abolition in *American Nineteenth Century History*, the *Canadian Review of American Studies*, and the *Pennsylvania Magazine of History and Biography*. Her books have been published by New York University Press, Oxford University Press, and the University Press of Florida. Meant as a general introduction to the topic of slavery and abolition in the Keystone State, this book offers a synthesis of works produced in this field from the early twentieth century to the present day. It calls attention to the importance of enslaved labor in establishing the prosperity that has benefited the state from the beginning and continues to do so today. In the end, *Slavery and Abolition in Pennsylvania* highlights the complexities of emancipation and the "First Reconstruction" in the antebellum North, presenting both a new look and a long-awaited synthesis on the topic. It explores the assumptions and realities of bondage and the quest to end it in the Quaker State.

We would like to thank our peer reviewers for their excellent feedback and the PHS editorial board for their sound guidance, especially that of Kristin O'Brassill-Kulfan. The work of the series is made possible by the financial commitment and leadership of the PHA Council. We are grateful to our friends at Temple University Press, who once again have worked their magic by turning a raw manuscript and some image files into the polished book that you now hold in your hands.

ACKNOWLEDGMENTS

THIS BOOK HAS TAKEN LONGER THAN I INTENDED, and I have racked up numerous debts in the time that I have worked on it. First, I would like to thank the University of Houston–Victoria (UHV) for the faculty development grant that funded my travel to the Pennsylvania State Archives. I also appreciate the funding that the university has provided for me to participate in the Pennsylvania Historical Association, Society for Historians of the Early American Republic, and Organization of American Historians conferences that brought me back to Pennsylvania to sneak in additional quick trips to the various archives, including the Library Company of Philadelphia, the Historical Society of Pennsylvania, the Pennsylvania State Archives, and Swarthmore College. UHV also provides excellent library support, and I especially want to thank Jean Mutschler for her research assistance and Lou Ellen Callarman for her amazing ability to get anything I needed through the interlibrary loan network. I could not have finished this work without their much-appreciated help. I also could not have finished without the patience and support of Provost Chance Glenn, who cared enough to ask about the project and understood when I needed to take time off to complete the revisions.

Writing history may seem like a solo act, but it is not. I am fortunate to have a number of friends in the profession to share ideas with and send photos of archival documents, and who encourage me when needed. I have been particularly lucky over the years to get to know an awesome group of historians through the Pennsylvania Historical Association, including Randall

Miller, Rachel Batch, Michael Birkner, Tina Hyduke, Janet Lindman, Linda Ries, Lauri Roffini, Ed Slavishak, and Diane Wenger. Also through the PHA I met my dear friend Allen Dieterich-Ward, who has patiently pushed me along with this project, and Karen Guenther, who suggested I take it on in the first place. There is no better community in the history world than that associated with the Pennsylvania Historical Association, and I am honored to be part of the family. I would especially like to thank my friend Cory James Young, another Pennsylvania historian whose work with *The Activist History Review* as well as his cutting-edge scholarship in the field of slavery, antislavery, and race in Pennsylvania is top notch. He read the full manuscript and provided careful and much-appreciated feedback. Nicholas Wood and Kristin O'Brassill-Kulfan offered excellent advice, as did the members of the editorial board of the *Pennsylvania History Series*. I am also grateful for the assistance of Emily Smith at the Library Company of Philadelphia and Sara Horowitz of Haverford Special Collections for helping me collect images for the book and Randy Pollard for allowing me to use an image he took of me as my author photo.

Of course, I feel the most gratitude, especially with a synthesis like this project, should go to the historians whose work on which I am building here. This is a strong field that includes some of the best historians out there. My largest debt goes to the pioneering work of Ira V. Brown. I was fortunate enough to correspond with Dr. Brown in the early 2000s while I worked on my *Pennsylvania Hall* book, and during that time he sent me a self-published manuscript called *Proclaim Liberty*. I have put it to great use here.

Finally, I owe a great deal to my family for their support and enthusiasm. Andy volunteered photography skills and equipment to copy images, most importantly the one of the Germantown House. Gracy read parts of the manuscript and offered advice, particularly on the introductory sections of the chapters. Joey offered the same enthusiastic support as always and made sure to find the time to ask about how the project was going, pushing me to finish, whether intending to or not. Bobby kept us all fed and kept me supplied with plenty of tea to get through the rough spots.

SLAVERY AND ABOLITION
IN PENNSYLVANIA

INTRODUCTION

WHEN SHE RAN AWAY, she had to conceal the one thing she had been trying hardest to hold on to—her identity. She had been kidnapped from her West African homeland and sold to light-skinned people that she thought might be evil spirits or even cannibals. After that, they chained her to people who did not speak her language and sent her across a body of water that seemed never to end. After that long, terrifying, and painful journey, they sold her in North America, where they tried to take away her identity as well. One part of that process was forcing her to go by "Phebe," a name she was still getting used to. She left Africa a valued part of an ethnic community and family and arrived across the ocean an outsider and a commodity.[1]

The people who claimed ownership of her cared not that she had a home, family, and community. They did not even try to understand her body art and the language she spoke when she tried to communicate. They just wanted her to work, and they used her unique characteristics as oddities to describe her in newspaper advertisements after she escaped. Her captor warned that she was a "cunning Wench" who would likely "wear a Handkerchief round her Head" to hide the "four large Negroe scars up and down her forehead." She would also hide her poor grasp of English by speaking fast. Despite the network of oppression that sought to re-kidnap her, "Phebe," whose real name nobody ever bothered to learn or record, managed to remain at large ten weeks after fleeing. One can only imagine the heartbreak she must have felt after being hunted down and forced into a life of slavery a second time.[2]

This photograph of a young woman in Surmi, Ethiopia, shows scars similar to the ones described on Phebe. This practice continues in some parts of Africa in the twenty-first century, and this particular image was taken in 2015. (Photo by Rod Waddington, Wikimedia Commons, CC BY-SA 2.0: https://creativecommons.org/licenses/by-sa/2.0/legalcode.)

Phebe, like many people who ended up enslaved in the mid-Atlantic region, was originally from West Africa—most likely part of the Asante, Benin, Tuareg, Ibo, Yoruba, or Senegambian group. Chances are, her kin placed the markings on her by scarring her face in a unique way that matched theirs. This was a custom that held cultural significance among many different groups and would also make it easier to find her way back to her people should she end up captured by an enemy nation or slave traders in Africa. Unfortunately, the marks could not help her get home from so far away. She now faced the reality of hard work for no pay, followed by an early death, an ocean and two continents away from the people she loved. In addition, her attempted escape now left her with the prospect of being beaten or sold into even worse circumstances.[3]

Telling the story of someone like Phebe remains difficult for historians. While the past few decades have shed light on enslavement and slavery in the South, much of the story of northern slavery remains hidden, especially when looking to understand it from the perspective of the humans who lived in bondage. For one matter, it remains challenging to find windows into their lives, since the historical record contains few specifics about how they lived and worked, much less what they felt and thought. Complicating matters even further is the long-held (and incorrect) notion that slavery in the North was "not so bad" or somehow "more humane" due to the presence of abolitionists. This holds most true for Pennsylvania, the state that passed the first abolition law in the new nation soon after the United States gained independence from England. The Quaker presence in Pennsylvania has also encouraged an oversimplified narrative that focuses on moral opposition to slavery and the system's early demise in the state. This false sense of moral superiority too often allows us to overlook the fact that slavery was ubiquitous and that there were many people who benefitted from it and fought to keep it, even as the abolition movement grew in the nineteenth century. It also hides the fact that antislavery sentiments too often grew from antiblack sentiments fed by fear and a desire for racial exclusion. It encourages a history that exonerates those who benefitted from human bondage and forced labor while downplaying the continuing legacy of slavery and racism, the scars of which continue to mar the nation's social and political landscape even today. It is time to correct this false narrative. The bottom line is that there was no safe place for Africans or black Americans in the United States in the slavery years, not even in the "free North" or the Quaker State, and it is time to come to terms with that and develop a more authentic understanding of the U.S. past.[4] Black and white Pennsylvanians need to know the full story in order to appreciate the historical collaboration that ended human bondage. They also need to understand the contributions black Americans made to Pennsylvania and the United States, and to understand the challenges they faced, and still face, in a society constructed for the benefit of whites.

The image of kindly Quakers ending slavery quickly out of the goodness of their hearts and with little resistance is one that must be replaced with a more authentic story of what really happened. That story must include a wide range of characters, including the Quakers who chose to keep enslaved laborers as well as those who fought against human bondage. It must also include black Americans like Phebe who refused to surrender to their plight and those of both colors who stood up for justice, acknowledged the wrong of owning human beings, and worked together to correct that wrong. Theirs was a fight led by people who knew that just because something is legal and accepted does not mean it is right. Though unpleasant, a true account must also tell the stories of those who clung to their fear, anger, and the resulting racist beliefs to fight against the tide of freedom.

The purpose of *Slavery and Abolition in Pennsylvania* is to tell the full and inclusive story and to bring to light the realities of both slavery and abolition in the state. Though short, this volume presents a long-awaited synthesis on the topic of slavery and antislavery in the state, revealing the complexities of both and exploring the assumptions and realities of bondage and the quest to end it in the Quaker State. Although Pennsylvania is known as the first state to end slavery, in reality it was simply the first state to put abolition in motion through law, but people remained enslaved in the state until the eve of the Civil War. Contrary to popular belief, that process was not a peaceful one, and abolitionists met tremendous backlash that often endangered their property and their lives. After slavery ended in the state, black and white activists continued to fight the system, hoping to spread freedom beyond the commonwealth's borders. That, too, brought dangerous backlash and resistance, not just from residents of other states but from Pennsylvanians as well.

Importantly, the fight for freedom did not end with the fight to end slavery. Certainly, owning oneself was an important first step to gaining liberty, but real freedom requires opportunity for true independence. Thus, it helps to think in the long term and view the fight against slavery as simply the first stage in a long civil rights movement that began in the colonial period and continues today.

Slavery and Abolition in Pennsylvania traces this movement from its beginning to the years immediately following the American Civil War. The first section explores the lives of people like Phebe—people who were robbed of their lives in Africa and forced across the Atlantic to the New World colonies, where they had to labor in difficult, often excruciating, work for no pay. It describes their work, their relations with those who believed they "owned" them, and their attempts to make the most of their situation by forging their own identity in any way they could. It also discusses their attempts to gain freedom, whether by "stealing" or buying themselves.

After examining slavery in Pennsylvania, the discussion turns to the complexities of the state's antislavery movement by examining the reasons different groups of Pennsylvanians opposed slavery and the various ways they proposed to end bondage and reconstruct Pennsylvania society. It also traces the backlash abolitionists and black Americans faced and the growth of anti-abolition sentiment and racism that followed the passage of the gradual abolition act and grew in tandem with new forms of antislavery that developed in the antebellum years. The final section traces the civil rights movement from the period of state reconstruction through the national reconstruction that occurred after the Civil War.

1

SLAVERY IN THE QUAKER STATE

ENSLAVED AFRICANS LIKE PHEBE began arriving in the mid-Atlantic as early as 1639. Some were brought directly from Africa, but the majority spent time in the Caribbean first. Most entered the region through Delaware River ports, the most prominent of which was Philadelphia. All in all, the northern states would benefit from colonial times to the present from a system of human bondage that was even more varied and complex than slavery in the South. The humans trapped in this system were made to participate in a complicated economy that relied on their forced labor in skilled and unskilled roles. It created a world in which white workers came to resent all black workers, slave or free. It planted the seeds of white prosperity and racism, leaving them to grow together in ways that continue to shape the region today.

While New England led the way in the colonial slave trade through its shipbuilding and shipping industries, New York and Philadelphia also thrived in the buying and selling of human beings. The earliest social and economic elites in the colonies gained their wealth and power through owning and trading in enslaved people, and the accumulated capital fostered economic development that laid the groundwork for the mid-Atlantic's prosperity. Thus, slavery fueled economic growth in the region in three ways: (1) through the trade in human beings, (2) through the unpaid toil of those commodified humans, and (3) through the collateral industries that grew alongside the slave trade, including shipbuilding and shipping. The resulting capital was then used to finance other enterprises, from distilleries to textile mills to universities. Given how tightly it was woven into just about every aspect of the economy, slavery was central to the region's prosperity from the beginning. The wealth generated allowed the richest of families in the mid-Atlantic to accumulate profits that would fuel the Industrial Revolution and, in turn, lead to even more money. That wealth would last for generations and provide investment capital that some continue to profit from in the twenty-first century.[1]

A number of prominent Pennsylvanians gained their wealth from participating in the slave trade. Perhaps the best known were Thomas Willing and Robert Morris. They, along with Thomas Riche, and the team of Garrett and George Meade, were the largest traders in the region. Collectively, these brokers sold well over half of the Africans purchased in the Delaware region. Others included Isaac Norris, Jonathan Dickinson, and Robert Ellis. These men, some of whom were Quakers, included slave sales as part of their regular business, selling people for cash or credit and sometimes even allowing for purchases on installment plans or through bartering. Sometimes they sold their human merchandise in private sales, but other times they relied on auctions. Trade in human lives was a complex business that required merchants

The London Coffee House and Philadelphia's Market House regularly hosted auctions in which enslaved humans could be bought and sold. Prospective buyers at the London Coffee House, located on the corner of Front and Market Streets, could relax and enjoy coffee while bidding on humans whose fate rested in their hands. (Image from the Library Company of Philadelphia.)

to facilitate the transactions, lawyers and scriveners to keep the records, brokers to execute the deals, and tavern keepers and auctioneers to host the sales.[2]

There was no social stigma to selling enslaved people, even when conducted by auction. Indeed, men involved in this trade often earned leading social and political roles locally, regionally, and nationally. Take, for example, Robert Morris and Thomas Willing. Morris was the founder of the Bank of North America and a member of the Continental Congress. Through his financial maneuvering, he played a central role in financing the revolutionary cause and getting the new nation on its feet, though he would find himself in debtors' prison later in life due to risky financial moves. Willing was president of the Bank of North America from 1781 to 1791 and the Bank of the United States from 1791 to 1807. He played an important role in developing the artisanal and mechanical communities of Philadelphia by helping to create the cash marketplace and promoting an environment protective of domestic trade. He also served as a judge, mayor, and assemblyman. Likely worth over a million dollars, Willing was probably the richest man in Philadelphia between the mid-1790s and the War of 1812. Once the slave trade was outlawed in Pennsylvania, Willing and Morris resorted to landing their human cargo in New Jersey and smuggling them into Pennsylvania.[3]

The People Who Were Bought and Sold

The people who became merchandise in the hands of slave traders arrived in the region after suffering tremendous humiliation, physical and emotional torture, and exposure to numerous deadly circumstances. Their ordeal began in Africa, whether they were taken as prisoners of war or captured during a raid launched specifically to gain slaves for the market. However they ended up in this situation, their capture was followed by an overland march to the African coast, where they were imprisoned in one of the slave fortresses to await their transport across the Atlantic.[4]

The movement of enslaved humans across the Atlantic is referred to as the "Middle Passage." This miserable voyage could take anywhere from one to six months, depending on weather conditions and the ship being used. During their transport across the ocean, enslaved people were often chained together and packed into the lower decks, too close to have any personal space or even lie down. Not knowing what to expect, they were terrified, and some committed suicide to avoid the fate that they feared awaited them across the ocean. Those who survived the passage spent months below deck in filth, among human waste and the remains of others who died during the journey. Because it sometimes took days for the crew to remove the bodies of the dead,

Elmina Castle is one of the most notorious fortresses on the African coast. Built by the Portuguese in 1482 on the Gold Coast, this fortress was seized by the Dutch in 1637, and they continued using it for the slave trade until 1814, at which point the British Empire took it over. It is now a UNESCO World Heritage Site in present-day Ghana. (By Johannes Vingboons, between 1665 and 1668, *Atlas Blaeu-Van der Hem*, 36:19, fol. 62–63 [16], Austrian National Library, Wikimedia Commons.)

and because of the filthy conditions in general, disease spread rampantly, and the leading causes of death on these ships were disease and starvation. Approximately 15 percent of the victims of this trade (nearly two million people) died at sea.[5]

Between 9.5 and 12 million Africans faced this nightmare, but only a small fraction were brought to the middle colonies. Most who ended up in the region did not come directly from Africa but instead had first spent years in the Caribbean being "seasoned" by slave owners there. They began arriving in the Dutch settlement on the Hudson River that would eventually become New York in 1626, just five years after the first white settlers arrived. Soon after, Africans were brought to the area that would eventually become Pennsylvania. Edward R. Turner, a pioneer in the state's African American history, found mention of a convict in 1639 being sentenced to "serve among the blacks" at South River.[6]

Quakers came to embrace the use of enslaved labor for the same reason as other colonists—the profit that derived from a stable labor source. Jean Soderlund, an expert in Quaker history, has pointed out that Quakers came to the

New World for two reasons: "the twin promise of religious freedom and economic prosperity." Focusing on the first of these reasons and overlooking the second has fed into an oversimplified argument that Quakers naturally opposed slavery because they believed in the concept of the "Inner Light," or the idea that all humans share the capability to be touched by the Holy Spirit and should thus be allowed the freedom to follow that calling. Instead, "religious belief and economic interest interacted" in the Quaker approach to slavery.[7]

Slavery was well established in the area when William Penn founded the colony in 1682. Penn purchased 150 Africans within two years of his arrival, though those were likely for resale. He kept at least twelve, including people named Sam, Sue, Yaff, Jack, and Peter, and neither he nor any other leader in colonial Pennsylvania made any real effort to prohibit the institution. His use of enslaved labor at his Pennsbury estate gave the system a sense of legitimacy, and others followed his example. Between 1682 and 1705 one in fifteen families in Philadelphia owned slaves. By 1767, 15 percent of Philadelphia's households owned enslaved workers. Despite the fact that the Society of Friends had begun to discourage slave owning by this point, Quakers made up a large number of these slaveholders. Historian Gary Nash has argued that "the rank and file of Philadelphia Friends" were willing to sacrifice their principles more readily than forgo the human labor needed to make a profit.[8]

Slavery in Pennsylvania

In the colonial period, most enslaved people in Pennsylvania lived in the southeastern part of the state, near Philadelphia, but the population spread westward toward the capital region and beyond by the early national period. Counties with the highest enslaved populations included Bucks, Chester, Lancaster, Montgomery, and York, but human bondage had spread to Columbia by 1726, Susquehanna by 1733, and Pittsburgh by 1759. Tax records show average holdings of one to two enslaved workers, except in Philadelphia, where the wealthier owned two to four. Iron masters generally held the most, with holdings of five or six in many cases.[9]

Given the diversified nature of the economy in the mid-Atlantic, slaves could be found in a wide range of occupations, with the iron industry being one of the most common, beginning as early as 1716. Beyond agriculture and iron, enslaved laborers in the North were used in a range of artisanal fields such as sail making, printing, shoemaking, clothes making, blacksmithing, baking, and carpentry. They also worked in the brick and candle making industries. The balanced growth of industry and agriculture facilitated by the changing seasons and different climates of the North led slavery in the

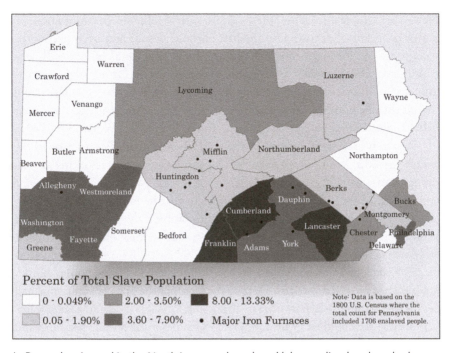

Percent of Total Slave Population

☐ 0 - 0.049%	▨ 2.00 - 3.50%	■ 8.00 - 13.33%
▨ 0.05 - 1.90%	▨ 3.60 - 7.90%	• Major Iron Furnaces

Note: Data is based on the 1800 U.S. Census where the total count for Pennsylvania included 1706 enslaved people.

In Pennsylvania, and in the North in general, enslaved laborers lived and worked primarily in small individual holdings on farms and in urban households. The largest use of enslaved labor in industry was in iron production, so the largest holdings could be found in the furnaces. (Map created by Jacob Wacker for this book.)

mid-Atlantic to develop in a way that it spread throughout the region's economy, rather than being isolated to agriculture. Enslaved labor was used by colonial leaders for private gain as well as for public works such as fortresses.[10]

Slavery grew out of white aversion to doing hard work for someone else's profit. An abundance of opportunity to buy their own land and start their own businesses left whites in the northern colonies unwilling to accept wage labor when they could reasonably attain an independent existence, so the region came to rely strongly on indentured servants and enslaved workers. The first preference of many was for indentured servants because in many cases it was assumed that Europeans would already have the necessary skills needed, and the whites who needed laborers were generally more comfortable working with other whites. However, the supply of indentured servants was dependent on "push factors" that would encourage Europeans to leave their home countries and "pull factors" that would draw them to the colonies. This led to an unstable market that faced interruption regularly, especially in times like the Seven Years' War, which interrupted the flow of indentured servants.

Many who did make it across the Atlantic chose to enlist in the armed forces. The resulting short supply of servants led the colonial assembly to warn Thomas Penn that "if the Possession of a bought Servant . . . is . . . rendered precarious . . . the Purchase, and Of Course the Importation, of Servants will be discouraged, and the People driven to the Necessity of providing themselves with Negroe Slaves, as the Property in them and their Service seems at present more secure." The English government persisted in offering potential servants more lucrative opportunities, continuing to draw them away and push colonists toward slavery. With so many opportunities in the New World, laboring for others rested on a compulsion that only enslaved Africans were subject to. Even if those with capital preferred white indentured labor, by late 1756 their best option for a steady and reliable labor supply was enslaved labor from Africa.[11]

After that, wealthy colonists in need of workers increasingly used forced labor to fill their needs. Slave importation in Pennsylvania had averaged about twenty per year in the 1740s and thirty a year in the early 1750s, but then it began to rise sharply. In the peak import year of 1762, as many as five hundred enslaved workers were brought to the colony, many directly from Africa. From 1763 to 1766, between one hundred and two hundred forced laborers were brought in annually. In 1767, there were almost fourteen hundred enslaved people serving masters in Philadelphia, making up one-twelfth of the city's population of sixteen thousand people. By 1780, there were six thousand enslaved laborers in the state, mostly in the southeastern part near Philadelphia in Bucks, Chester, Lancaster, Montgomery, and York Counties. Masters came from the ranks of the elite as well as merchants, shopkeepers, artisans, and those in the maritime industry.[12]

Profiting from Unpaid Labor

Those who switched to bound labor found a solid return for their investment. Whereas indentured servants were protected by contracts that limited their terms of service, enslaved workers enjoyed no such protection and were owned forever once bought. In most cases, enslaved laborers had similar training and skills as white workers, especially since most of the people bought in Pennsylvania had spent time being trained, or "seasoned," in the Caribbean. Enslaved people were also less likely to run away or join the militia than white servants because of the difficulty in hiding among the general population. Finally, white servants, unlike enslaved blacks, were armed and expected to participate in the colonial militias, so those who relied on white workers lost their labor to the armed forces in times of war or conflict, while slave owners had a guar-

The Chew summer home, Cliveden, located in Germantown, Pennsylvania. (Courtesy of the Library Company of Philadelphia.)

anteed labor force even during war. Those who relied on the labor of others often preferred white laborers, but enslaved laborers provided a more reliable and steady workforce.[13]

Once the English took the middle region of the Atlantic coast from the Dutch, some began to build manors that were heavily dependent for their upkeep on enslaved laborers and began to decrease the rights of those bound workers. One of the most famous manors in Pennsylvania, besides Pennsbury, was Cliveden, built by Pennsylvania chief justice Benjamin Chew, the Penn family lawyer. He arrived in Philadelphia in 1754 and held various provincial offices during his lifetime, including attorney general, the governor's counsel, and chief justice of the Pennsylvania Supreme Court. One of the largest slaveholders in Pennsylvania, Chew had as many as sixteen to twenty-five forced laborers living at Cliveden at one time or another between 1768 and 1831.[14]

Forming Community in Slavery and Freedom

According to historian Darold Wax, Africans brought to colonial Pennsylvania were selected "specifically for the local market, with the region's labor requirements firmly in mind." Boys and girls ages twelve to sixteen were preferred, and the importation of an equal number of women and men resulted in a "nearly balanced sex ratio." The earliest arrivals especially found it difficult to form unique communities with other Africans because of the wide distribution of enslaved laborers. This led to a heightened degree of assimilation and "few opportunities to engage in collective activities." New arrivals, like Phebe, were often distinguished by their difficulty with the English language, and it is unclear how they were treated by the established black population, though Wax tends to believe they found support. Most new arrivals, he argues, "settled quietly and as best they could into their new role," learning "the configurations of the slave system" as quickly as they could. After locating "the soft spots in the institutional structure," like Phebe, they "appropriated physical and psychological space" where they could. While many may have tried to maintain as much of their African heritage as possible, ultimately "their numbers were too few, their contacts with kinsmen too limited" to do so.[15]

The first enslaved people to arrive in this region would later be freed and serve as the nucleus for a free black community, but this opportunity for status mobility did not last long, as lifetime slavery was established in the mid-Atlantic by the 1640s. Codification of slavery in the region took place gradually, beginning in 1694 with a punitive slave code that forbade enslaved flight and included laws against enslaved people carrying guns, even for hunting. That same year officials gave all white men the power to arrest suspected escaped slaves found more than five miles from their home. A year later the government of New Jersey established special courts for enslaved people. By the early 1700s, according to historian James Gigantino, colonial governments throughout the region had adopted slave codes that "delineated who qualified as a slave, established punishment (usually severe) for criminal offenses committed by slaves, and placed restrictions on slave movements and rights." By this point, treatment of enslaved people was harsh and violent, with masters whipping, raping, and castrating them and sometimes going so far as to burn them at the stake.[16]

Slavery was institutionalized in Pennsylvania in three stages. First, between 1682 and 1700, legislation was passed that made slavery a lifelong condition, though slavery and servitude were still nearly the same in practice. Between 1700 and 1726, slavery was made more distinct from servitude by two laws that collectively made up the slave code of Pennsylvania. The 1700 law subjected black Pennsylvanians to different courts and imposed on them different punishments for murder, buggery, burglary, and rape of a white woman. This law also restricted black movement and forbade marriage between whites and blacks. Between 1726 and 1780, minor adjustments prescribed corporal punishment for blacks for crimes that would bring fines for whites. With these laws, historian Edgar J. McManus explains, Pennsylvania joined a process that put blacks in every colony in a "dehumanizing descent into the chattel status peculiar to American slavery." This status included being listed among taxable property and included in wills, along with tools, livestock, and other household goods.[17]

The legal code also imposed a second-class status on free blacks. Laws against interracial marriage prescribed that free blacks who entered into sexual relations with whites were to be sold as servants for seven years and that free blacks who married whites were to be sold into lifelong slavery. The same law stipulated that children from these unions would have to serve thirty-one years, making them "term slaves." This condition of semi-slavery became de facto heritable, as people sought to hold the children of term slaves in the same condition as their mothers. There were also vagrancy laws that re-enslaved any black "fit and able to work" who refused to do so. Finally, Pennsylvania laws forbade blacks from carrying pistols, clubs, or muskets under penalty of twenty-one lashes and prohibited blacks from participating in militia training, relegating even free blacks to menial civic tasks such as clearing and repairing highways.[18]

Likely due to the proximity of the South, the middle colonies placed the strongest restrictions on black mobility. Pennsylvania forbade blacks from traveling more than ten miles from home without a pass, from gathering in groups of more than four, and from venturing on the streets at night. Enslaved people who were found in the streets on Sundays in Philadelphia without a pass were given thirty-nine lashes, and their owners were charged the cost of their detention and flogging. Those accused of theft were punished with flogging, branding with a *T* on the forehead, and deportation. Suspected arsonists faced hanging. All of these punishments were meted out through special courts that did not include the right to trial by jury. To prevent owners from trying to protect their human property to avoid financial loss, Pennsylvania offered unlimited compensation to owners whose slaves were killed in the course of punishment. The law did impose some limitations on masters, forbidding them from abandoning or deliberately killing their human property or maiming them in the exercise of discipline. Technically, it was illegal to murder a slave, but since a master had unlimited punishment rights, it was almost impossible to prove deliberate murder.[19]

WHEN PHEBE RAN AWAY FROM THE PERSON who claimed to own her in 1763, she was boldly fighting a well-entrenched system of human bondage that had the legal and social support of most white Pennsylvanians. By running away, she was choosing to "steal herself" from her master, so her resistance was illegal, both in her insubordination and in her attempt to claim valuable property, even if that property was her own life and liberty. Like most who chose this path of resistance, she would eventually be caught and returned to lifelong slavery in a foreign land far from home. The one thing that would forever remain her own was the time she remained at large. Nobody will ever know what she did during those ten weeks, what kind of help she may have found within the black community, or how she managed to remain free, even for that short period. Those secrets went with her to the grave, but the historical record can tell much about the world in which she lived under slavery in colonial Pennsylvania.

2

LIFE IN BONDAGE

WHEN CUFF DIX RAN AWAY in June of 1776, the man who claimed the right to his life, liberty, and labor described the marks that distinguished him. According to Mark Bird, his slave had "an iron ring in one of his ears" that was "large enough to receive the small end of a pipe stem." Unlike Phebe, whose facial markings likely had been placed by family and friends seeking to designate her as one of their own, Cuff's marks were placed by an owner who sought to label him as a perpetual outsider, one who would forever be the property of another. Both had marks of belonging, but the meanings of that belonging were worlds apart.

Like so many others in his situation, Cuff Dix remained determined to belong to nobody. According to Bird, his escaped slave's name was simply Cuff, so perhaps Dix's first act of defiance was to claim a last name for himself. After that, he tried repeatedly to reclaim his autonomy by running away from Bird's iron forge at Birdsboro in Chester County. The first instance on record occurred on May 8, 1775, when he fled and managed to remain at large for six months before being jailed in Chester that November. He had likely tried unsuccessfully to escape before that because, according to the advertisement, he left wearing an iron collar.

Bird, who had established Hopewell Furnace in 1770–1771 and was one of the largest landowners in Berks County, described Dix as a "most excellent hammerman" and an "active well made fellow" whose work he admittedly depended a great deal on. Dix, however, realized the value of his own labor and escaped to find paid work for his own benefit. After Bird claimed him

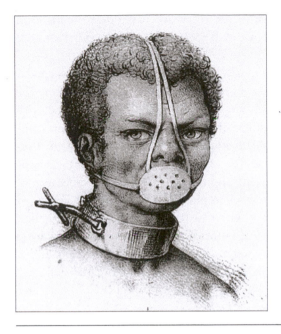

Slave collars were used to punish runaways and to try to prevent them from repeating the offense of "stealing themselves" from their owner. The image shows an enslaved person being silenced by one device while also wearing a collar. Other "slave collars" or "runaway collars" had spikes of various lengths and bars that stretched out in ways that would get caught on brush and vegetation. Some even had bells attached. (This image is in the public domain, originally appearing in Jacques Étienne Victor Arago, *Souvenirs d' un aveugle: Voyage autour du monde* [M. J. Arago, 1839], 119.)

from the jail in Chester in late 1775, Dix absconded again and spent most of the next summer working for someone in Chester County. Perhaps that escape occurred after Bird's attempt to mark him by disfiguring his ear, because an ad placed in July 1776 mentions the marking for the first time. That ad describes him as a frequent runaway who could be identified by a tendency to stutter, should he somehow manage to hide the disfigurement to his ear. Dix was also aware of the political climate around him, as Bird speculated that he might have run off this time to join Lord Dunmore, the English governor of Virginia, who had promised freedom to enslaved people who would join the British in their efforts to put down the colonial rebellion.[1]

Slavery in Country and City

The life Dix fought so hard to escape was that of enslavement in an industrial area of Pennsylvania. Due to the mixed economy, slavery in the mid-Atlantic was varied and included agricultural work, industrial and artisanal labor, and commercial and domestic jobs in towns and cities. Enslaved Pennsylvanians labored in iron forges, tanneries, shipyards, and farms. Among them were skilled artisans such as bakers, masons, carpenters, shoemakers, butchers, tailors, millers, hatters, coopers, clockmakers, barbers, and brewers. Indeed, there was likely no profession that did not include enslaved labor at some point. The conditions of their daily lives varied according to the industry in which they labored, the region in which they lived, and the proclivities of their particular master.[2]

The mid-Atlantic is a region of diversity. It has varied topography and a climate that has supported a range of industrial pursuits from early on. The middle colonies, particularly Pennsylvania, were also culturally diverse, with a variety of Native groups coexisting before European contact. Settlers coming from England, Wales, Ireland, Scotland, Germany, France, Spain, Sweden, and Holland displaced these first inhabitants beginning in the seventeenth century. The ethnic diversity, along with the religious tolerance of founder William Penn, fostered a religious pluralism as well. Settlers included Quakers, Presbyterians, Lutherans, German Reformed, Baptists, Catholics, Jews, Anglicans, and adherents to a number of smaller religious sects from throughout Europe. The settlers were of diverse economic circumstances, including wealthy landowners, artisans, laborers, small landholders, and servants. In addition to these were the captives brought from the Caribbean and Africa who were forced into lives of slavery.[3]

Slavery in the region was also diverse. The people who found themselves enslaved there often had little in common with each other. They were brought from different regions of Africa and had different backgrounds, a situation that discouraged them from creating bonds of unity. The conditions of their daily lives were also quite varied.

Though Pennsylvania's agricultural productivity was among the highest in English North America, the plantation system never took root there because northern colonial development centered around small farming, manufacturing, and commerce. This meant that, instead of living separately in slave quarters, enslaved laborers in the agricultural sector shared living quarters with those who held them in bondage. This situation denied them the modicum of freedom provided by separate quarters and gave masters an additional level of control over them. They lived in small groups since most northern slaveholders held one or two bound laborers, and they ate the same food as their masters, often at the same table. They worked side by side with their masters in the fields and in blacksmith shops on the farms. Historians have recently argued that the lack of separate living spaces has made it easier to erase the past, intentionally or not, and forget that slavery even existed in the North. Unlike in the South, where tourists can visit plantations and see the "slave quarters," in the North such structures are not part of the physical landscape.[4]

The second most common place to find enslaved laborers in Pennsylvania was in the domestic space. In both urban and rural households, enslaved women washed, ironed, tended children, and served meals. They also sewed the family's clothing and drove buggies and carts. Some worked as market women and body servants for their enslavers. Their presence brought respect and social status to the families they served. Women who worked in this space faced the added challenge of near-constant scrutiny from whites.[5]

Enslaved Pennsylvanians could also be found contributing to every phase of the economy. In cities like Philadelphia, they were an important part of the artisan class, working as bakers, tailors, weavers, coopers, millers, masons, goldsmiths, carpenters, cabinetmakers, glazers, and shoemakers. Indispensable to the maritime industry, they also worked in the shipbuilding trades as sail-makers, rope makers, caulkers, shipwrights, and anchor makers. They participated in commerce as well as manufacturing, working as sailors on their masters' ships and serving as buyers of merchandise for their masters' stores. Indeed, the versatility of their work brought them into competition with white workers and fostered an atmosphere of resentment. This jealousy led white artisans and workers to appeal to the colonial assembly to pass laws against black labor in 1707 and 1737, and lawmakers' failure to do so only heightened white anger and resentment toward blacks, both free and enslaved.[6]

Bound labor was also used extensively in industry. Industrialists like Mark Bird commonly used enslaved laborers, whether they owned them or rented them from others, a process called "hiring," even though payment went to the enslaver rather than the enslaved. According to one study, between 1765 and 1787, 30 percent of proprietors of commercial industries owned slaves, and over 30 percent of enslaved workers in the mid-Atlantic were hired by businessmen who needed to supplement their own bound and free work-forces. This meant that nearly two-thirds of enslaved workers in the region were employed at one time or another in a commercial operation. Of eighty commercial operations examined, 65 percent owned enslaved workers, 84 percent hired them, and only 13 percent operated without the work of enslaved laborers.[7]

The wages paid to slaveholders for the use of enslaved workers were very close to those paid to free workers. Since the wages went to the enslaver rather than the worker, this made slavery even more profitable. The cost of an enslaved worker could be recovered in fewer than six years, and in nine years even the cost of a slave's daily maintenance would be recovered by these wages. Costs were recouped even faster by masters who owned skilled laborers.[8]

This system was made even more lucrative by its ability to help slave owners evade taxes. Slave owners who hired out their slaves only counted the ones who were currently on their property for assessment purposes, conveniently forgetting to count those who were hired out when inventorying their taxable property. Tax assessors infrequently verified inventories, and the frequency with which enslaved workers were moved around made it unlikely they would catch the misreporting, even if they did try to verify holdings. County commissioners generally knew about this sleight of hand but overlooked it because most of them were slave owners or were related to slave owners and benefited directly or indirectly themselves from such creative accounting.[9] The hiring-out system, and the money raised from the flexible nature of slavery, created community investment in enslavement by allowing a wide range of people to profit from the forced labor of others.

Enslaved Labor in the Iron Industry

The most common industry to employ hired enslaved workers was the iron industry. This practice began in 1675 when New Jersey Quaker and merchant Lewis Morris used enslaved labor in the construction of a forge and then relied on enslaved laborers to do the bulk of the work once the site was in operation. Enslaved laborers worked regularly at Charming Forge as hammermen between 1767 and 1775 and at Pine Forge as woodcutters in 1773. They worked at Union Forge to cut wood on an annual basis between 1785 and 1789. Women began working in the forges in 1732 in multiple facets of iron production. In general, iron companies owned between four and twelve enslaved laborers, and furnaces with fully equipped forges required the most full-time workers.

As a result, the largest slaveholdings in Pennsylvania were generally found in the iron industry. In 1780, the four largest slaveholders in Berks County were ironmasters. Collectively they owned nearly half of the slaves registered in the county. In York, Chester, and Lancaster Counties, the tax lists for 1779, 1780, and 1783 show ironmasters owning almost a quarter of the 824 slaves in the area. Furnaces and forges in southeastern Pennsylvania and New Jersey were the "largest single employers of both waged and enslaved labor" throughout the eighteenth century, creating a space where indentured servitude, slavery, and free labor existed side by side. Hired slaves like Cuff Dix and white laborers worked together and interacted closely in the forges and furnaces.[10]

Through its use of enslaved labor, the Pennsylvania iron industry led the way in instituting a type of worker control that has been used to divide workers along racial lines and foster racism ever since. According to historian John Bezis-Selfa, owners of forges and furnaces in the mid-Atlantic "acquired and exploited slaves as an integral part of a strategy to discipline white wage workers and maximize proprietary control." They turned to slavery to make themselves less dependent on the whims of free white workers and to drive down the costs of labor. Law and social custom also allowed them to supervise enslaved workers more closely and punish them more harshly than white workers. The resulting racial tensions were similar to those that continue to plague the working class and hamper worker solidarity to this day. Finally, an enslaved worker served for life and did not have the freedom to leave to find better conditions. As an added bonus, enslaved West Africans brought with them sophisticated metalworking expertise that they could put to use in Pennsylvania's forges and foundries.[11]

Community Networks and Resistance

In addition to being employed more often in industrial work, enslaved northerners were more likely than their southern counterparts to live in cities. City living offered distinct advantages. They gave enslaved Pennsylvanians opportunities to form family bonds and social networks. In cities like Philadelphia, enslaved and free blacks interacted with each other in marketplaces and worship services, establishing kinship networks. Those who lived in rural areas sometimes had the chance to learn about and participate in these networks when their masters took them to the city for business purposes. Those who worked on ships were able to enjoy extensive Atlantic networks that allowed them to learn about each other's cultures and share information, some of which was useful in their efforts to pursue freedom. According to historian James Gigantino, the networks they created allowed enslaved Pennsylvanians "to develop their own culture, social customs, and exercise their own religion," creating an underground world "beyond the control of white masters" so that they could interact with each other on a daily basis, form romantic ties and family connections, and sustain what they could of their African cultures and traditions. These networks also allowed them to organize in hopes of resisting. They used every opportunity they could to enjoy some degree of the agency and freedom they dreamed of.[12]

Throughout the colonies, enslaved people resisted at every chance. Some committed suicide, and a smaller number murdered their captors, generally by poisoning them. Some women committed abortion or infanticide to prevent future generations from suffering enslavement. In rare cases, such as the 1712 and 1741 uprisings in New York or the 1734 conspiracy in New Jersey, they revolted in groups, always with deadly results that left innocent blacks murdered in the face of white terror and backlash. More commonly, they resisted simply by expressing as much autonomy as they could. One famous example is the Pinkster Festival, where they dressed up like Europeans, mocked enslavers, told stories, gave political speeches, enjoyed festivities with loved ones, and bought and sold goods they had made. Throughout the year, in the city and in the countryside alike, they participated in work stoppages and ran away.[13]

As the countless advertisements in northern newspapers illustrate, enslaved people in all regions most commonly resisted by trying to run away and build lives of their own. Between 1728 and the outbreak of the American Revolution, Benjamin Franklin's *Pennsylvania Gazette* ran ads for 783 runaways and notices of 193 people who had been jailed as suspected fugitives. Three of every four of those had escaped from the mid-Atlantic colonies of Pennsylvania, New Jersey, and Delaware. One in five escaped from nearby Maryland. The typical runaway resembled Cuff Dix, male and in his mid-twenties, though women also escaped when they could. Most of them were born in North America. Some were skilled workers and others were unskilled. Most ran away between April and October and in response to a specific event, generally hoping to avoid punishment or being sold. Many ran away to return home after being sold. According to McManus, "even the most favored, docile bondsmen would defect when the chances of gaining freedom seemed favorable."[14]

Successful runaways posed the most serious threat to the system of slavery, and masters knew it. As McManus explains, "every successful escape set off tremors that undermined discipline and encouraged others to defect." Knowing this, masters refused to give up, doggedly chasing people for several years after they left. This meant that even successful runaways faced the constant threat of being captured. It also meant that free blacks lived in constant fear of being claimed as runaways since there was no way to protect themselves from erroneous and false claims as to their freedom. Instead, the sweeping powers given to authorities to arrest and detain people suspected of being runaways could easily be, and often were, used to drag free blacks into lives of enslavement. Take, for example, a man named Tom who was detained in New Castle in January of 1763. According to jailor Alexander Harvey, Tom, who was dressed in "a good blue Coat, with metal Buttons, Great Coat, Leather Breeches, good Shoes and Stockings, &c," claimed to be a tenant of Philadelphia merchant Thomas Riche. Certainly, the attire he wore was not typical of an enslaved person, and he not only insisted on his free status but offered the name of his landlord as a witness to his freedom. Even so, the jailor held him for four weeks to wait for a master to claim him. If not claimed, Tom was to be sold to cover the charges of his incarceration.[15]

Tom's story illustrates the precarious nature of freedom in the North. Early historians made the erroneous claim that northern slavery was more benign than southern. They pointed to adequate feeding and clothing as evidence to support their claims. Recent works, however, have corrected this error and shown that, regardless of location, the master-slave relationship was by nature predicated on physical force and violence and that violence and terror spread beyond slavery and into society as a whole.[16]

Punishment and Social Control

Whites kept a close watch over blacks, enslaved and free, and passed special laws to keep them under as much control as possible. These Black Codes were fairly easily enforced in rural areas because of social distance and physical isolation. Authorities in cities such as Philadelphia, however, encountered logistical difficulties in their attempts to police urban life since it was almost impossible in a crowded city to consult every master on the legitimacy of his slaves' presence in busy thoroughfares. As a result, the laws were applied to black people regardless of their status, creating a race-based social system.[17]

Race-based laws led to race-based punishments that wove oppression deep into the fabric of life and culture in the mid-Atlantic. Some have argued that northern slavery lacked the systematic barbarism found on the southern plantations, but others have pointed out that cruel and unusual punishment was employed in both regions. Others have shown that masters in the middle states could be just as harsh as those in the South, whipping, raping, and castrating the men and women they enslaved. Mid-Atlantic masters sometimes even burned enslaved people at the stake to instill fear and enforce discipline. Throughout North America, slavery was a system that inherently rested on brutality and oppression. The inhumane treatment used to uphold race-based chattel slavery fostered a way of thinking among whites that made it easy to transfer their treatment of the enslaved to free blacks.[18]

Despite the odds, some black residents of the mid-Atlantic managed to gain their freedom through escape. Others managed to pay for their freedom with money they earned by working during what little free time they had. Still others were able to capitalize on a growing antislavery sentiment that began to spread throughout Pennsylvania in the late 1700s, especially as the colonies came closer to war with England. As the political climate heated, slaveholders began to fear that enslaved blacks would enlist in loyalist militias and thus provide the nucleus of an armed rebellion. One enslaved man in Bucks County fed into this fear in 1776 by declaring his intentions to "burn the houses and kill the women" as they tried to escape. Others heard about offers like that of Virginia's royal governor Lord Dunmore to grant slaves their freedom if they fought on the side of the British.[19]

Indeed, that is exactly what Mark Bird speculated Cuff Dix had done. Perhaps Dix's June 1776 escape worked, because when Bird registered the eighteen enslaved people he claimed to own in 1780, Cuff Dix was not one of them. Whether he joined Dunmore or not, Dix's appreciation of his own value and strength, his hatred of bondage, and his awareness of a growing antislavery sentiment among his white neighbors fueled his sustained resistance and may well have resulted in his eventual freedom.[20]

––––––––––

BEFORE TURNING TO THE STORY OF FREEDOM, it is important to understand the full implications of slavery in the North, the mid-Atlantic, and Pennsylvania. To begin with, slave ownership was more widespread in all three than people have generally realized. The labor of enslaved people broke the land for farming, grew the crops that fed black and white settlers and workers in the region, extracted raw material from the earth, and helped to build the industries that led the region to prosperity. In addition to the benefits of direct ownership of forced labor, Pennsylvania profited from participation in the slave trade. That trade fed the growing shipping industry and brought vast amounts of capital into the colony. This capital was used to build the early infrastructure that fueled further industrial and commercial development. Through actual slave ownership and the indirect benefits of the capital that the trade brought, Pennsylvanians built a thriving industrial base that gave Pennsylvania economic and commercial advantages for generations. Because slavery did not leave visible landmarks like slave quarters and plantations, and because its demise did not leave the kind of economic scars seen later in the South, it is easy to forget that it ever existed in the North, including in Pennsylvania. But it did. And the benefits it brought, though often invisible to those who would rather not see them, were crucial to the region's continuing prosperity.

Whether working for the shortsighted goal of his own freedom or the broader goal of ending human bondage, Cuff Dix was an abolitionist. He was one sort of abolitionist—the kind working from the strongest motivation of all. But it would ultimately take the combined efforts of many types of abolitionists—political, social, moral/religious, and immediately interested—to end slavery first in Pennsylvania and later in the United States. Phebe, Cuff Dix, and others who resisted enslavement forced whites, whether slaveholders or not, to acknowledge the evil of human bondage and, in some cases, to join the fight against it. Black resistance was the beginning, but it would take the efforts of a wide coalition of forces to take on the interests of proslavery Pennsylvanians. After a century of resistance, their efforts would ultimately pay off in the form of the first U.S. abolition law, passed in 1780 in the face of continued opposition.

3

PENNSYLVANIA'S
EARLY ABOLITION MOVEMENT

THE SPIRIT OF REVOLUTION was in the air as Joshua Richards signed the contracts. He and his associates in the Bucks Quarterly Meeting had taken on a major project to cleanse their religious community of the taint of slavery. Before he could join the other members of the Visiting Committee, he had to first do what he would be asking of others, so he prepared legal documents to free the two people he had been claiming as property. Once he did that, he and the other members of the committee met at his home, where they developed an action plan. The first step of their process involved acquiring a list of the names of slave owners in their community. To that list, committee members added the names and ages of the people enslaved in each household and noted whether each could read or write and what skills they were known to have. Finally, they included each master's apparent disposition toward the idea of parting with their human property.

Armed with their list, these Bucks County Quakers began to visit their neighbors and try to convince them to release the people they held in bondage. Perhaps the most interesting case they worked during the nine years they met between March 1776 and February 1785 was that of Elizabeth Warden. They visited with her twelve times and made slow and incremental progress. She strung them along on the first two visits, leading them to believe she was considering their request, but on the third visit she freed only one person, a sixty-nine-year-old woman. Given that the woman was likely at the end of her productive time, this was no great sacrifice, but it opened a door for Warden, who freed five more people in 1777. She told the committee she would free no more, yet they persisted and convinced her to free five more people when they visited her a tenth time. She freed the last of the twelve captives in 1781. Warden's story is one of a long struggle that led to ultimate victory and, in that sense, it serves as a metaphor for the antislavery movement in Pennsylvania in general. Slavery would end in the state only through the combined efforts of many determined people, but one of the most persistent and insistent groups was the Society of Friends, or Quakers. Working county by county on slaveholders like Warden, their "quiet and undemonstrative way" helped push for the abolition of slavery in Pennsylvania. The Bucks County Visiting Committee alone visited at least twenty-six different slave owners and rescued fifty-two people by securing their legal manumission.[1]

Quakers and Early Pennsylvania Abolition

Antislavery activity began in Pennsylvania long before the Visiting Committees began meeting in the 1770s. Historians generally attribute this resistance to the colony's Quaker mission of peace and nonviolence. Focused on the idea of all humans having an "Inner Light" that could be touched by the Holy Spirit at any time, the Society of Friends developed an ethical code that, when followed logically, easily led to conclusions of human equality, conclusions that could make it difficult to mistreat, much less own, another person. Deeply opposed to violence, the Society of Friends naturally had reservations about slavery, and members began to consider the system soon after coming together as an organized body in the 1650s. When George Fox, the founder of the society, traveled to Barbados to share his group's interpretation of Christianity, he saw firsthand the horrors of human bondage and called on Quakers to consider that God was equally concerned with enslaved people as with others. Thus, he argued, slave owners should treat those they had enslaved mildly and free them after a period of servitude. Though Quakers were the main slaveholders in the first years of Pennsylvania's settlement, a growing number of them began to see slavery as a violation of the Golden Rule and to question how it was possible to reconcile with Christ's teachings the practice of holding human beings in bondage.[2] Quakers alone, however, could not have defeated slavery. As the stories of people like Phebe and Cuff Dix illustrate, slavery's defeat began with black resistance. After that, German colonists joined the effort to convince the Quakers to give up, and then fight against, slavery.

The problem was that not everyone wanted to follow their faith to its logical conclusion when that conclusion could mean inconvenience and economic loss. The antislavery Quakers had a long fight ahead, first within the Society of Friends, and then beyond it. They had to stop people from importing and selling human beings and then convince them to free the people already held captive in the colony. These were two different matters. It would take a century for resistance to grow strong enough to lead to legal action against slavery. The first formal protest against slavery was issued by German Quakers in 1688, but the trade would not be banned among the Society of Friends as a whole until the 1750s. Quakers banned slave owning in the 1770s, but legal prohibition for all Pennsylvanians would not come until 1780.[3]

A formal protest issued by a small group of German Quakers in Germantown in 1688 planted the seeds of the Quaker antislavery movement. This Germantown Petition, sometimes called the Germantown Protest, was the first organized effort to cleanse the Society of Friends from the sin of slavery. It was written by Mennonite exiles who had joined the Society of Friends and moved to Pennsylvania in 1685. The main author of the petition, Francis Daniel Pastorius, was a lawyer who had served at different times as mayor, clerk, and keeper of records in Germantown, as well as in the Provincial Assembly in 1687 and 1691. He was also a schoolmaster and authored what has been described as "probably the first schoolbook written in Pennsylvania." Dutch settlers Garret Hendricks, Derick Up de Graeff, and Abraham Up de Graeff also signed the petition. In a nutshell, it argued that "the oppression of blacks was no more acceptable than the oppression of Quakers in Europe, that the existence of slaves in Pennsylvania deterred potential European settlers from emigration and that slave revolts posed a major threat to Quaker welfare."[4]

The petition was presented to the Quaker Monthly Meeting in Abington but was deemed "too weighty" and sent to the Philadelphia Quarterly Meeting, who then sent it to the Philadelphia Yearly Meeting, the top meeting in Pennsylvania. There it was rejected and set aside until it was rediscovered in 1844. From the point of its rediscovery to the present, it has been regarded as the "seed of the Quaker abolitionist movement."[5]

The petition's German influences are perhaps more significant than its Quaker influences. Many historians have pointed to German reluctance to own slaves from the outset, while English Quakers owned slaves from the beginning of Pennsylvania's settlement. Only 17 of the 521 slaveholders identified by Gary Nash in his study of slaveholding in Philadelphia were German. He attributes the low number as much to "an aversion to slaveholding" among German immigrants as to economic reasons. In general, the Germans remained outsiders and refused to adopt English practices. From the moment they arrived in the colony they set themselves apart, insisting that they be given land together and not dispersed throughout the settlement. In 1689, they managed to acquire a charter to create their own borough.[6]

The Germantown Petition was set aside after being rejected by the Philadelphia Yearly Meeting in the late 1680s, to be rediscovered during the height of the antislavery movement in 1844. Celebrated as the foundational document of the Quaker abolition movement, it was set aside once more in the mid-1800s and then rediscovered a second time in 2006 in a vault in Arch Street Meeting House, the home of the Philadelphia Yearly Meeting, where it had been stored along with Cadwallader Morgan's 1690 protest. (Image courtesy of Haverford College, Quaker and Special Collections, Haverford, Pennsylvania.)

The Germantown settlers had what historian Katharine Gerbner described as a "fundamentally different perception of black slaves" than did their English neighbors. They "conceived of blacks as the social and spiritual equals of whites," arguing that it was no different to enslave whites than blacks and that there should be no difference in how the Golden Rule was applied. They also compared the oppression of blacks to the oppression of Quakers and Mennonites and questioned the assumption shared by most English that blacks were spiritually and socially inferior to whites.[7]

While the Germantown Protest presented moral arguments and appealed to religious conscience, it also argued that ending the slave trade would be necessary to white self-interest. The petitioners began by arguing that slavery was morally wrong because it violated the Golden Rule and forced creatures of God to commit adultery by tearing families apart and making people live together in forced situations in the New World. It also brought to the colony a moral taint that discouraged European immigration. Finally, it was a dangerous system that put both white souls and white lives in peril. Enslaving human beings angered God, who would likely bring forth vengeance at some point. It also angered those whose freedom had been stolen, and they too might employ violence at some point to avenge the wrongs committed against them. Should this happen, the petitioners asked, would the Quaker colonists be willing to violate their nonviolent principles and defend themselves in the face of insurrection? They asked if those they had robbed of their liberty did not have "as much right to fight for their freedom, as you have to keep them slaves?"[8]

Five years later, a group of dissenting Quakers led by George Keith issued another document that used moral and religious arguments while also appealing to white self-interest. This protest, *An Exhortation and Caution to Friends Concerning Buying or Keeping of Negroes* (1693) was the first antislavery protest printed and circulated in the colonies. After Keith's disownment by the Quaker establishment, a splinter group calling themselves "Christian Quakers" adopted his *Exhortation and Caution*, which offered five reasons to oppose slavery. First, Keith claimed that slavery violated the Golden Rule. He also claimed that buying slaves meant buying stolen goods. Quoting Deuteronomy and Exodus, he argued against the cruel treatment of slaves and the dismantling of their families. He pointed out that Jesus's strictures against oppressing servants, whether brethren or stranger, made slaveholding a sin, and he warned that any riches acquired through the slave trade would draw God's wrath. He used Scripture to make the point that all humans are created by God, and that God would eventually seek justice for His abused children. To avoid divine retribution, Quakers must cease buying enslaved people unless to free them. Those who already owned humans should "teach them to read, and give them a Christian Education," and then set them at liberty after they had worked long enough to repay their purchase price or, in the case of babies born under slavery, the cost of their upbringing.[9]

William Southeby, another Quaker abolitionist, brought together previous arguments while offering some original thoughts of his own in a 1696 speech that finally caught the attention of the Philadelphia Yearly Meeting and helped convince them to discourage the slave trade. In 1712, he challenged not only the Society of Friends but also the Pennsylvania legislature to abolish slavery. By 1714, he became so vocal that his Monthly Meeting threatened to disown him over his antislavery efforts. Southeby had immigrated to Maryland as a Catholic but had converted to the Quaker faith and moved to Philadelphia in 1686. Two years later he was elected to the Pennsylvania Assembly. Though neither wealthy nor elite, he managed to gain enough respect within the Society of Friends to represent the Philadelphia Quarterly Meeting at the Yearly Meeting from 1695 to 1709 and was chosen to serve on Yearly Meeting committees. He was especially active in Philadelphia Monthly Meetings. In 1696, he became the first to call for a law banning slave importation, and in 1712 he asked the colonial legislature to emancipate all enslaved people.[10]

Southeby's protest inspired another Quaker, Cadwallader Morgan, to issue a statement the same year. Morgan took a practical stance and focused even more on the dangers slavery could bring to whites, and while Southeby's work gained some attention, it was Morgan's that drew results. He focused on the ways in which slavery could harm white families, offering images of blacks raping white women and of slaves revolting against Pennsylvania slaveholders, as they had done in Barbados in 1649, 1674–1675, and 1692. The Philadelphia Yearly Meeting offered an official warning that was clearly influenced by Morgan and Southeby, though they chose to focus on Morgan's emphasis on self-preservation over Southeby's focus on liberty. The appeal of Morgan's warnings over the focus on the Golden Rule illustrates the strength of self-interest over moral arguments. The Society of Friends' statement represented a compromise that discouraged but did not ban the slave trade and included no enforcement sanctions. Unable to take away the demand for enslaved workers, Southeby began to target the supply by appealing to Quakers in Barbados to stop sending enslaved people to Pennsylvania.[11]

The Colonial Assembly and the Slave Trade

Frustrated with the slow action of Quakers, Southeby took his crusade into the public sphere and petitioned the Pennsylvania Assembly for emancipation

in 1712. This pushed the discussion beyond the meetinghouse and into society at large, but it still left him disappointed. The Quaker-dominated assembly deemed it inexpedient to seek emancipation. However, after the New York slave uprising of 1712 illustrated the point about the dangers of slavery to whites, they did impose a twenty-pound duty on slave imports, but it was annulled by the British crown. The London Yearly Meeting also denounced slave importation but refused to completely disallow slavery. Frustrated, Southeby became more vehement in his protests and began publishing papers without permission of the Quaker Overseers of the Press. Quaker leaders ordered him to stop, but he refused and continued to petition the assembly until his death in 1722.[12]

As Southeby learned, ending human trafficking would be easier than securing freedom for the enslaved, primarily because it included an element of self-interest that advocates could play upon to gain support. In 1711, the Chester Monthly Meeting petitioned the Philadelphia Yearly Meeting to forbid Friends from buying imported slaves, and the Philadelphia Meeting responded by asking the London Yearly Meeting about slave importation in 1712. The London group responded that they foresaw a day in which "it would be found dangerous to have brought [slaves] into the country." The Chester Quarterly Meeting petitioned the Yearly Meeting again in 1715 and 1716, but since 60 percent of the Yearly Meeting leaders owned enslaved people at that point, they would only "caution" Quakers to avoid buying slaves. Between 1730 and 1737, Quakers came around to the idea of ceasing further importation, and by 1740 importation among Friends had stopped.[13] They were still not ready to call for manumission.

The Quaker-led colonial government tried multiple times to take measures to stop the trade by placing import duties on enslaved laborers. They began in 1700 with a tax of twenty shillings. In 1712, they increased the duty to twenty pounds, but the English government annulled the duties to protect the Royal African Company. Edgar J. McManus attributes the 1712 duty to the effects of one of the insurrection attempts in New York, and it is clear that the resulting fear of revolt did indeed win the support of more non-Quakers to the anti-importation cause, yet importation continued and reached its peak in 1760. A year later, however, the Pennsylvania Assembly placed a ten-pound duty on each enslaved person imported into the colony, finally stopping the flow of new slaves being brought in. After that, the existing population failed to reproduce its numbers and began to die off, leading to a resulting decline in political support for slavery.[14]

The end of the Seven Years' War resulted in a restoration of the supply of white indentured servants, with German and Scotch-Irish immigration returning almost to prewar levels. By the end of 1770, the slave trade had "all but ceased" in the colony, and Pennsylvanians turned back to white indentured servants to satisfy their labor needs. In 1775, the Pennsylvania Provincial Convention convinced the Pennsylvania Assembly to prohibit importation altogether. Even so, it would take another fight altogether to convince those who already held enslaved laborers to divest themselves of that property and restore them to their liberty.[15]

From Ending the Trade to Seeking Emancipation

Though it took longer to win, the fight against enslavement began about the same time as the fight against the slave trade. The Germantown group, Keith, and Southeby had argued for manumission, and individual Quakers had begun to develop the argument that slave owning was sinful as early as the 1690s. They started to free their enslaved laborers at the turn of the eighteenth century, with the first recorded case occurring in 1701, when Lydia Wade freed her enslaved laborers in Chester County. William Penn wrote a will that same year that would have freed his enslaved laborers upon his death, but it seems to have been superseded by another will that did not follow up on this promise. Southeby petitioned the Pennsylvania Assembly for general emancipation in 1712, but the legislature, while complying, did not make manumission easy, passing a law in 1725–1726 that required thirty-pound security bonds to ensure those they freed would not become a burden to the community. Under this law, black children, whether emancipated or born free, could be bound out as apprentices without their parents' consent. Free blacks deemed vagrants could be indentured, and a black man who married a white woman could be sold into slavery.[16]

One of the most outspoken critics of slavery in this early period was Ralph Sandiford. After seeing the suffering of enslaved people in the West Indies, he produced two antislavery works, *A Brief Examination of the Practice of the Times* (1729) and *Mystery of Iniquity* (1730). These works were deemed "inflammatory," and church and civic leaders tried to stop their publication. Collectively they present a strong and forceful indictment of slavery that was ahead of its time and resulted in Sandiford's disownment and ostracism by Quakers and the Philadelphia community at large. Sandiford freed his slaves the year he died and others, like John Baldwin of Chester, followed suit by freeing theirs in their wills.[17]

Even more controversial than Sandiford was Benjamin Lay, a man of tiny stature but huge personality. Born to Quaker parents in Colchester, England, Lay came to Philadelphia after living in Barbados, where he was exposed to

Portrait of Benjamin Lay. (Image courtesy of the National Portrait Gallery.)

the horrors of human enslavement. In 1737, he labeled slavery a sin in his *All Slave Keepers, That Keep the Innocent in Bondage, Apostates*. He was notorious throughout Pennsylvania Quaker circles not just for his written work but also for the stunts he pulled to gain attention for his cause. Already a curious sight at four feet, seven inches tall and with a humped back, he drew further attention to himself and his mission by fasting for almost a month, kidnapping the child of a local slaveholder to show him how slaves felt when their children were taken from them, and stabbing a Bible with a sword to release red juice all over a meeting of Quaker congregants. He was deemed radical due to his zealousness, his vegetarianism, and his choice to live in a cave outside the city.[18]

Between 1750 and 1780, manumission among Quakers grew increasingly frequent. John Woolman argued that everyone was guilty of sin in a society that permitted injustices like slavery, and thus everyone would equally suffer the consequences. He prodded the Yearly Meeting to exclude Friends who bought or sold slaves from Meetings for Business and to "refuse their contributions as tainted money." Thanks to pressure from Woolman and others, the London Yearly Meeting expressed clear opposition to any connection to slavery in 1757, and the Philadelphia Yearly Meeting followed in 1758. That year, the Quaker establishment agreed to advise Friends to free their slaves and to refuse to allow those who continued to hold people in slavery to participate in the Society of Friends' affairs. Monthly Meetings began to partially disown Friends who imported, bought, or sold enslaved people. While not banning slaveholding outright, the society denounced slavery unequivocally at this point and urged Friends to manumit those they held in bondage. To achieve this end, Woolman and others were appointed to Visiting Committees to convince slaveholders to follow the official advice.[19] The Bucks Quarterly Visiting Committee led by Joshua Richards and his friends was part of this effort.

Unlike those before him, Woolman had the official sanction of the Quaker establishment. His works were published with the approval of, and funding by, the Overseers of the Press of Philadelphia Yearly Meeting. Like others before him, Woolman appealed to the Golden Rule and other biblical teachings to reach the conscience of his fellow Quakers. A young adult during the time of Lay's agitation, Woolman decided that behavior most Friends deemed radical and offensive would alienate possible followers, so he chose a softer approach. He hoped to convince Quaker leaders to disown slaveholders, but when they refused, he compromised by convincing them to create the Visiting Committees and using them to apply moral pressure to convince slaveholders to change their ways.

Historians agree that the Pennsylvania Yearly Meeting's 1758 appointment of Visiting Committees signified the beginning of the end of slavery among their ranks. Without officially disowning slaveholders, they still made it clear that owning slaves was no longer acceptable because it was inconsistent with the Society of Friends' ideas about how people should treat each other. The official pronouncements against slavery by the Society of Friends, and the visitations that followed, left every Quaker slaveholder in a moral conundrum as they worked to reconcile economic interest with religious ideology. In addition to the 52 enslaved people rescued through the efforts of the Bucks County Committee, the Philadelphia Quarterly Meeting secured the freedom of 125 people, though many of those were children who would remain under indentured servitude until they reached the age of twenty-one for males or eighteen for females. After the Visiting Committees had a chance to win slave owners over to the cause, those who still refused to free their captives were disowned under a new policy adopted in 1775, illustrating the persuasive and gradual, but persistent, nature of the process Woolman was willing to accept in order to eventually achieve his goals.[20]

Woolman's balance between pressing for immediate action and accepting a slower pace of change out of concern for the unity of his religious society illustrates the mild manner of Quaker reform. The contrast between the styles of Lay and Woolman also illustrates a tension that would remain part of the antislavery movement throughout its existence—the disagreement over whether radical or mild tactics would do more for the advancement of the cause. Woolman also introduced a key tactic that would inform the antislavery work of generations to come when he refused to use any goods produced by enslaved labor.[21]

THE NEXT STEP after purging slavery from the Society of Friends would be to take the antislavery momentum into broader Pennsylvania society and convince non-Quaker neighbors to do the right thing and release their human captives. In the wake of war, the movement gained traction among Pennsylvanians beyond the Society of Friends. Most of these early abolitionists, whether Quaker or not, focused on respectable agitation, reliance on the laws and the courts, and acceptance of whatever incremental gains they could achieve in their persistent efforts to end enslavement in the state. Quakers would remain the majority in the movement, but their new allies would play important roles in passing the new nation's first antislavery law.

4

ABOLITION BEYOND THE QUAKERS

IN ONE OF THE MOST INFLUENTIAL TRACTS produced during the anti-slavery movement, Anthony Benezet tried to force his readers to realize the humanity of people like Phebe and Cuff Dix, as well as all the other black Americans who still toiled in slavery or worked hard to scrape out a living under conditions of precarious freedom. Whites had begun to try to justify enslavement by arguing that Africans lacked the emotional depth of Europeans, were lazy, and came from societies that accepted slavery as a natural condition. Benezet used travel narratives written by explorers and merchants to dispel these popular myths and misperceptions by describing African life honestly and realistically. He admitted that Africans engaged in slavery, but he described just how different African slavery was from that in the New World. Because he approached the task like a scholar and relied on firsthand accounts, he produced a work that would gain acceptance as one of the first credible sources for African history told from a Eurocentric perspective. Just as important, it would become, according to David Crosby, the editor of Benezet's complete writings, "a kind of bible for later abolitionists."[1]

Through Benezet's eyes, the barren and barbaric Africa of popular culture was replaced by a comfortable land, well "calculated for affording the necessary comforts of life to its inhabitants." The people, when viewed through lenses other than those of a slaveholder trying to justify his own barbarity, "manifest themselves to be a humane, sociable people, whose faculties are as capable of improvement as those of other people." Contrary to the false narratives circulated by enslavers and slaveholders, who described African society as backward and underdeveloped, Benezet described the economics and government as "in many respects commendable."[2]

If Africans acted differently once they were in the Americas, Benezet argued, it was because they found themselves in bondage in a society that, though claiming to be "enlightened" and "Christian," left them "little opportunity or encouragement to exert and improve their natural talents." Lacking the incentives of "wealth, . . . authority, or honor" those who toiled under slavery for the benefit of others faced "no reasonable prospect" of any personal gain and were left with "neither inducement or opportunity to exert . . . their natural capacities . . . to advantage." Benezet argued this would not be the case if they "stood upon an equal footing with the white people."[3]

Because enslavement had adversely affected most whites' opinions of blacks, even many who supported ending the slave trade opposed freeing the people who had already been brought into slavery. They argued that, in the absence of masters, the former slaves would be lazy and end up on the public dole. Some also insisted that if blacks were free of white control, they would take the opportunity to seek revenge. Benezet disagreed. As he addressed these concerns, he laid out a comprehensive plan to end slavery and provide equal opportunities for the former victims.

Benezet's plan sought to provide freedom and create conditions for equality. It began with prohibition of the slave trade, the one component many white Pennsylvanians could agree on. The second step involved freeing enslaved people "after serving so long as may appear to be equitable." Once freed, they would be "enrolled in the county courts, and be obliged to be a resident during a certain number of years within the said county under the care of the overseers of the poor." The program also included education for adults and children. Finally, Benezet wanted to provide incentives in a form that amounted to land reparations by assigning "a small tract of land . . . to every Negro family" and requiring them to live on and cultivate the property. When not working their land, the freedpeople could work for whites for wages. Benezet expressed optimism that "both planters and tradesmen would be plentifully supplied with cheerful and willing-minded laborers" who would be allowed to benefit from their own hard work.[4]

Benezet's Quest to Prove African Humanity

The challenge for Benezet was selling his plan to his neighbors. Most Quakers, at least, had come to support ending the slave trade, so he needed to convince them of the merits of ending bondage and then accepting free blacks. Of course, to make it all work, he had to draw in allies from beyond the Society

Anthony Benezet was instrumental in ending slavery as well as working to ensure that the freed would be able to enjoy their liberty as citizens in the new nation, particularly through education. (From *Historical, Poetical and Pictorial American Scenes*, by J. W. Barber, 1850, Wikimedia Commons.)

of Friends and sell them on the plan as well. Benezet's greatest innovation was to shift the argument away from religious and philosophical principles, focusing instead on empirical facts about Africans in Africa to prove that they were humans who had been kidnapped from happy and productive homes and were entitled to the same natural rights as any other humans. He also focused on the brutal behavior of slave owners and the unremitting toil enslaved laborers faced at their hands.[5]

Benezet's *Epistle of Caution and Advice* emphasized the violence and cruelty used to capture and enslave people and warned that slavery hardened the hearts of whites and left their souls incapable of engaging with God's "spirit of love, meekness and charity." He pointed out how disingenuous it was for people who rejected war to buy humans who were prisoners of war or who had been violently stolen from their families, and he reminded readers of the Golden Rule. He asked those who already held slaves to treat them in accordance with God's love, keeping families together and preparing enslaved people for freedom. While others focused on stopping importation, Benezet set his sights on emancipation, prompting biographer Maurice Jackson to refer to him as "the father of Atlantic abolition." He fought not only for black freedom but also for equality. More than an abolitionist, Jackson argues, he was a "genuine social reformer." His efforts led the Philadelphia Yearly Meeting to accept the idea of freedom as a natural right and to virtually endorse immediate emancipation of slaves, and his work took abolition beyond the Society of Friends.[6]

After Quakers finally endorsed a policy to disown those among them who did not free their enslaved workers in 1775, emancipation took off. The first manumissions in Abington Meeting were recorded that March, and between then and the end of 1777, twenty-six manumissions were recorded. These were gradual, with men serving to age twenty-one and women to age eighteen, but the process of freedom was underway, and Quakers had created their own system of gradual emancipation that would shape the statewide law of 1780.[7]

An anonymous author using the name "Justice and Humanity" brought some of Benezet's arguments into the public eye again in March 1775 in a *Philadelphia Journal* article titled "African Slavery in America." Like Benezet, this author relied on the words of slave traders to argue that Africans were being taken from fertile countries where they were industrious farmers who lived plentiful lives and were "averse to war" until Europeans intruded upon their world, introducing alcohol and encouraging them to fight each other and capture their neighbors to be sold in the New World. Also like Benezet, he mentioned enslaved people's "natural right" to freedom and condemned separation of families. Finally, he pointed to the hypocrisy of American revolutionary rhetoric that protested white colonists' metaphorical enslavement by the British while they were literally keeping Africans enslaved.[8]

The Emergence of the
Pennsylvania Abolition Society (PAS)

One month after this article appeared, a group of reformers met in Philadelphia's Sun Tavern on Second Street and founded the first iteration of what would be the Pennsylvania Abolition Society (PAS). The saga that led to this momentous meeting began in 1773, when Dinah Nevil, a Philadelphia woman described by contemporaries as "an Indian," was being claimed as a slave despite her assertion that she and her children were free. To protect Nevil and other Pennsylvanians from being held in slavery under false pretenses, ten Philadelphia men, most of whom were Quakers, met at the tavern on April 14, 1775, to form the Pennsylvania Society for Promoting the Abolition of Slavery, for the Relief of Free Negros Unlawfully Held in Bondage, and for Improving the Condition of the African Race. Benezet took the lead in calling this group together and attended the meeting. They discussed five cases of people they believed were being illegally held in slavery, including Nevil. While the mayor intervened and sent Nevil and her children to the workhouse for safekeeping, the group worked to devise a plan to take her case to the courts. The new society adopted a constitution and held further meetings in 1775. Twenty-four men attended one or more of these meetings, and they planned to meet the next February but were interrupted by the events of the American Revolution and would not meet formally again until February of 1784. They lost Nevil's case, but they hoped to prevent future incidents like hers, especially since there were thousands of free blacks in Pennsylvania who could feasibly face similar threats of being kidnapped and sold into slavery.

From the beginning, the society took the leading role in petitioning legislatures to abolish slavery and urging courts to declare slavery illegal. When these efforts failed, the society appealed to individual slaveholders to free their captives. Some members bought enslaved people to free them, and others led fundraising initiatives to help enslaved people buy themselves. The society used both words and money to help people gain their freedom, employing lawyers to prosecute freedom cases. Equally important, it worked to protect free blacks and prevent their unlawful enslavement through any means, including kidnapping.[9]

The American Revolution put the Pennsylvania Abolition Society's work on hold, but it did not stop the progress of emancipation. Manumissions continued as the war raged on, and the Quakers held to their promise to disown members who persisted in holding people in slavery. In 1776, the Yearly Meeting disowned slaveholders. After this resolution, the work of abolition among the Society of Friends was practically complete.[10]

Another Quaker, Warner Mifflin of Virginia and Delaware, drew on Benezet's inspiration. He not only tracked down people he had sold before 1774, purchasing them and freeing them, he also paid those he had previously kept in bondage if they wished to remain on his estate and work the land. He and his father went from holding significant enslaved labor forces to becoming two of the most vocal abolitionists south of Philadelphia. They reached beyond their Quaker network and tried to bring Presbyterians and Methodists into the antislavery cause, having little success among the former but making some progress with the latter. Mifflin even tried to convince Benjamin Chew, his wife's second cousin and the owner of the largest plantation in Kent County, of the immorality of owning human beings. According to biographer Gary Nash, however, "neither the appeals of Quaker reformers such as Mifflin nor revolutionary pamphleteers could soften the heart of the man who became the presiding judge of Pennsylvania's supreme court."[11]

The Call for Restitution

The inspiration Mifflin drew from Benezet was evident in his work for what would, in the twenty-first century, be called "reparations" for black Americans. Mifflin, however, referred to it as "restitution." He advocated providing freed people cash payments and access to land in a shared crop arrangement. After freeing those he had held in bondage, he brought a group of them together to ask what they suggested would constitute a fair system of repayment, and they collectively arrived at the terms of compensation.[12]

Neither Benezet nor Mifflin were the first to consider the merits of "restitution," or reparations. In Wilmington, Delaware, David Ferris had pushed for restitution since 1767, asking slaveholders to support the elderly and provide "liberally" for younger people they had freed. At about the same time, John Woolman and his brother Abner were raising similar issues in New Jersey. Abner argued that profits made by enslaved laborers should be shared with those workers upon their freedom, and John argued that the children of enslaved people who had worked into old age should be compensated for their parents' labor. British abolitionist Granville Sharp had made similar arguments to Anthony Benezet, maintaining that American farmers should provide the freed with homes and small farms, describing a system that sounded like sharecropping and resembled the arrangement Mifflin and his former slaves would arrive at. All of these ideas, however, came from people who did not own human property and thus had no capital at stake in the debate. What made Mifflin fairly unique is that he did face pecuniary loss, yet he did more than discuss the need for restitution.[13]

When he was unable to gain the support of the Quaker establishment in his quest for restitution, Mifflin shifted focus to his kinship network, putting pressure on relatives to follow his example. He managed to pressure several relatives and neighbors to provide payments of various amounts to people they had once held as slaves. By 1783, he was able to report an increased disposition among former slaveholders to do justice to those they had freed. He continued this effort until 1786, with mixed results.[14]

Victory through Legislative Action

Though the restitution movement was limited in influence, the abolition movement managed to spread beyond the confines of the Society of Friends through legislative action against slavery. Opponents of human bondage sent two petitions to the Pennsylvania Assembly in 1776 calling for manumission to be made easier. By 1778, the sentiment favoring legislative action had spread, and leaders took notice. Quakers lost their power in the governments of Pennsylvania and New Jersey during the Revolution, due to their opposition to war, so during the formation of the new nation, the Society of Friends' role was limited to pressuring state and federal leaders.[15] Securing allies beyond the Society of Friends became even more crucial as the fight against slavery entered the statehouse. Fortunately, at this point it gained strong support from Presbyterian legislator George Bryan.

In 1778, the executive council of the Pennsylvania Assembly, under Bryan's leadership as acting president, submitted a bill to the assembly that would have provided for the manumission of infants born to enslaved women and prevented all future importation of enslaved people. It offered no plan to free adults currently held in slavery, describing most of them as "scarcely competent of freedom." The assembly did not legislate even the moderate version of abolition proposed by the council at this point, but it did agree to discourage importation.[16]

Bryan and his allies continued their efforts. In 1779, the council declared slavery inconsistent with the new nation's fight for freedom from Great Britain. Calling slavery "highly detrimental to morality, industry, and the arts," the assembly argued that people fighting for their own freedom should be willing to grant freedom to others and added that abolition would be a good way to thank God for his help during the Revolutionary War. A proposed bill provided that black males born after the law passed would be freed at age twenty-one and females would be freed at age eighteen. Meanwhile, they were to be treated as slaves for a term, remaining in bondage with their mothers' owners until they reached the age of freedom. The assembly adjourned before acting on the bill. Supporters sent petitions to the legislature and letters to the newspapers. Benezet personally visited every legislator. Late in 1779, the *Pennsylvania Gazette* published the text of the proposed bill. Following public debate, the assembly voted, and on March 1, 1780, passed a modified "Act for the Gradual Abolition of Slavery." This was the first abolition act in the new United States.[17]

In its final version, the act provided for gradual abolition, freeing children born after its passage, but only after they reached adulthood at the age of twenty-eight. It left those already in bondage to remain in slavery, but it required that they be registered within eight months and that their names, the name and occupation of the professed owner, the name of their place of residence, and their age and sex be recorded. Those not registered would be freed. Those who were registered became term slaves and would be entitled to the same relief in cases of mistreatment and given freedom dues. Enslaved people brought into the state from other areas could only be held six months or until they reached age twenty-eight, unless they were domestic servants held by members of Congress from other states. Pennsylvania slaves who ran away within the state were expected to be treated as absconding indentured servants would be. The law also made all slave owners responsible to town overseers of the poor for the proper care of their slaves, requiring them to post a bond of thirty pounds on each manumitted person to provide for their care in the case of indigence. The law included a section that made null and void earlier laws that supported racial discrimination, repealing a law that required blacks to be tried in separate courts without juries. It also ended the separate punishments instituted in that law, and it repealed another law that had made interracial marriage illegal and had forbidden blacks from meeting together.[18]

Limitations of Victory

Despite what seemed like a victory, the law had serious limitations. It contained too many loopholes, was easily evaded, and was gradual. As historian Andrew Diemer explains, it "freed no one immediately; it merely stipulated that all enslaved children born after March 1, 1780, would be freed upon their 28th birthday." Those born before "would remain in bondage perpetually, and those who were legally entitled to their freedom under this law found that their masters could too often circumvent it by transporting children or pregnant women south." Greedy masters also registered the children of term-enslaved women as term slaves themselves, profiting off the labor of yet another generation.[19]

Indeed, legal loopholes and illegal disregard of gradual abolition laws fostered an incredibly profitable internal slave trade that, according to James Gigantino, allowed slaveholders to transform enslaved people "from personal property to independent market commodities." As Edward Baptist has shown, this booming trade created conditions for enslaved people that amounted to a "second Middle Passage," as they were dragged by foot on long, painful journeys to newly settled territories in the South and West to grow cotton. This slave trade also generated the capital that would make the United States an economic and industrial powerhouse by the mid-1800s.[20]

Slaveholders visiting the state could bring enslaved people and keep them with them for six months at a time. This was particularly an issue in Philadelphia, the nation's capital from 1790 to 1800, because southern congressmen and other government leaders took advantage of this ability. Enslaved people sometimes tried to escape by blending in with the city's free black population. The most famous escape case was one of the few that ended in victory for the enslaved person. It occurred when Ona Judge, a woman claimed by George Washington, absconded while being kept in the city during Washington's presidential term. Most enslaved people, unlike Judge, were captured and returned to bondage, and this tense atmosphere of slave hunting and capture also affected free blacks because it made the threat of kidnapping a daily reality. It did not help that the 1780 law contained a fugitive slave clause seven years before the federal government would demand such a concession. Despite the legal end to slavery, then, the status of the freed remained ambiguous, and many found their freedom threatened or taken away entirely.[21]

Given the number of opportunities to recuperate their losses, for the most part, white Pennsylvanians accepted the end of enslavement in their state and worked to make the transition as easy on themselves as possible. Even those who did not participate in the interstate trade turned manumission into a commercial endeavor whenever they could, profiting by allowing some enslaved people to buy their own freedom. They struck deals with other enslaved workers to grant them freedom after they completed specific jobs or worked for an agreed-upon amount of time. Realizing the inevitability of losing the enslaved people they claimed as their property, many did what they could to get as much money as possible out of the arrangement. Many who chose to free the people they held in bondage maintained a sense of entitlement, expecting gratitude and deference from their former captives.[22]

Many historians agree that, despite almost a century of antislavery agitation by the Society of Friends, it was ultimately the American Revolution that undermined northern slavery. This was made possible for several reasons. For one matter, black Americans like Cuff Dix seized the opportunity to take their fate into their own hands and participate in the conflict on both sides, earning their freedom from the British and from the Americans. Just as important, the Revolution resulted in the rhetoric of liberty and self-determination that highlighted the hypocrisy of slaveholding.[23] This rhetoric converged with the antislavery sentiment that had begun to grow among Quakers and drew support from leaders of other religious persuasions, like George Bryan. The result was the first abolition law in the new nation. How well that law would work would depend on how willing white Pennsylvanians would be to go beyond abolition and truly accept the freedom and equality of their black neighbors.

Some historians have argued that the end of slavery in Pennsylvania was a victory of ideology over economic interest. They point to Quaker beliefs in the Inner Light and their pacifism, which opposed the harsh practices involved in gaining victims for the slave trade. They also point to Quakers' strong belief in the Golden Rule and their refusal to accept interpretations of Bible passages as proslavery, as well as their emphasis on the importance of family and their concern with the plight of the unfortunate. Others focus more on the revolutionary ideas and rhetoric that grew out of the American Revolution. They point to the hypocrisy of fighting for freedom from Britain while denying freedom to black Americans. Still others have pointed out that abolition was only possible in the state due to a lack of strong economic need for it in the region. While the economic need for enslaved labor was not as strong in the middle states as it was in the South, the bottom line is that relinquishing enslaved laborers came with costs. Gary Nash and Jean Soderlund have argued that emancipation was "a tug of war between ideological commitments and economic interests" and that ideology won. They are right to some extent. After all, more slaveholders could have sold their enslaved laborers to the South and made money rather than freeing them, but most chose not to and accepted the financial loss.[24]

Even so, the gradual nature of abolition in Pennsylvania advantaged slaveholders by minimizing their losses as much as possible and allowing them to recuperate as much as they could financially by keeping their enslaved laborers as long as they could or charging them ransom in exchange for their freedom. This amounted to reparations for the enslaver rather than the enslaved. The courts and legislature further coddled slaveholders by aiding in the process of stalling freedom, consistently refusing to move beyond gradualism and adopt total and complete abolition until 1847.

Black women suffered the most from the limitations of Pennsylvania's gradual abolition. They were generally the last to receive their freedom because domestic servants were often kept the full term of indenture while male laborers were released and allowed to find paid employment. Their ties to their children, who were often in apprenticeships of their own, made women less likely to run away, so they generally suffered their own indentures until they expired. According to Erica Armstrong Dunbar, though, they used the indenture period to "recreate themselves and their families, carving a space for themselves as semifree people who used friends and family, the Pennsylvania Abolition Society, and the Court of Common Pleas to gain some control over their contracts and over their lives." They worked to shape their indenture contracts and to hold their masters to the agreed-upon terms. Once they gained freedom, they worked to help others.[25]

JUST AS WOOLMAN served as a bridge between the movement to end slavery among Friends and the effort to outlaw it in the state entirely, Benezet bridged the gap between ending slavery in Pennsylvania and reconstructing society to make room for those freed from bondage. Though his reparations plan was never adopted, he continued throughout the remainder of his life to fight for fair opportunities for freedpeople. Benezet and the PAS would continue working to protect black Americans from kidnappers and to help them secure their freedom through the courts by exploiting loopholes in the law. They would also work alongside leaders of the black community to provide education for black children and job opportunities for black adults. Abolitionists of both colors wanted to take their movement beyond state borders, but they realized that they would first need to reconstruct Pennsylvania society to show that abolition could work. They would have to do this despite growing opposition and conservative efforts to take back the abolition law.

Whether they held enslaved people or not, most whites resented the financial and social losses that came with the end of slavery. Not only would they be unable to continue exploiting the labor of others for their own financial gain, they also lost formal control over the social lives of people they had grown quite accustomed to "owning." It was the loss of social control that bothered many whites, and nonslaveholders in particular found it hard to accept the end of human bondage for reasons that were more social than economic. Generations of living in a society in which most blacks were enslaved had left most whites with racist ideas that made them unwilling to see free blacks as their equals. Therein would lie the failure to accept true freedom.

5

THE FIRST RECONSTRUCTION

MOST OFTEN, laws are changed not by dramatic acts but by quiet violations, slow erosion, and piecemeal repeal. Some Pennsylvania slaveholders planned to do exactly that with the abolition law. First, they refused to register their slaves, but that backfired because the new law provided immediate freedom for the people they had not registered, and enslaved people soon learned of this and spread the word among themselves. Then they managed to get a more conservative state legislature elected in 1780 and appealed to the new leaders to help them regain their human property. The new legislators agreed that the law was "imprudent" and "premature" and argued that it would cause problems with the South and weaken the Union, especially in times of war. They also registered displeasure over the idea that it would give Pennsylvania blacks the right to vote and to hold office. They hoped to chip away at the law, and they focused first on re-enslavement and longer terms of service for people whose masters had failed to register them. At the urging of the new members, the Pennsylvania Assembly began to consider revising the law and extending the registration period to January 1782, creating the very real possibility that some people who had tasted freedom would be forced back into bondage. As would be the pattern for generations to follow, white abolitionists and the black community joined efforts to fight this development. While white abolitionists and lawyers sprang into action to fight the battle in court, black Pennsylvanians took their case to the public.[1]

A man named Cato sent an impassioned plea to the *Freeman's Journal*.

He and his children had gained their freedom through the registration loophole and now faced being returned to bondage, so he begged readers to understand just how torturous this would be. He argued that a law to hang people like himself would be more merciful than the proposal to re-enslave them, "for many of our masters would treat us with unheard of barbarity for daring to take advantage (as we have done) of the law made in our favor." Slavery had been hard enough to bear before, but "having tasted the sweets of *freedom*, we should now be miserable indeed." He then pointed out that re-enslavement would be hypocritical, given the words used in the opening clause of the abolition law. He repeated the previous legislature's assertion that the king of Great Britain had planted slavery in the colonies and that Americans, once free of British rule, had used their newly earned privilege to follow God's guidance and show gratitude for His support by extending liberty to those held in bondage. He quoted the previous legislature: "We esteem it a particular blessing granted to us, that we are enabled this day to add one more step to universal civilization, by removing as much as possible the sorrows of those, who have lived in *undeserved* bondage and from which, by the assumed authority of the kings of Great Britain, no effectual legal relief could be obtained."[2]

Thanks to the combined efforts of black Americans like Cato and white Quakers, especially those in the Pennsylvania Abolition Society, the legislature decided to vote against repeal, and future revision measures failed to gain serious support in the assembly. Though the law provided gradual emancipation that would bring only eventual freedom to people born into slavery after the law had been passed, it included loopholes like the registration law, and black and white abolitionists were ever vigilant in using those loopholes whenever they could to bring more immediate freedom to anyone who qualified. They also worked together to protect the newly freed from re-enslavement and abuse and to help them create new lives for themselves after emancipation.

Abolitionists who called for immediate action and historians alike have argued that Quakers and gradualists were "half-way" abolitionists, but the record simply does not bear this assertion.[3] Stealthy work, faith in the courts and the legal system, and quieter tactics may have made early abolitionists appear less threatening than those who followed them, but their work was just as bold and controversial. More importantly, their sustained efforts mirrored those of their opponents, but to opposite effect: slowly but surely eroding the opposition in the long war against human bondage throughout the United States.

Pennsylvania's First Reconstruction

Once the groundwork was set for the legal end of slavery, white Pennsylvanians had a choice to make. They could accept black freedom graciously or put up barriers to limit it as much as possible. Elite whites continued to value the economic and cultural ties they shared with southern elites and to welcome slave owners to share space in their cultural venues, such as churches, universities, and other public facilities. They resented the idea of having to share those spaces with blacks. Working-class whites were angered that they would have to compete for jobs with free black neighbors. Both groups harbored fears that their children would become socially and sexually involved with black Americans once the bonds of slavery were removed. Instead of accepting the freed into Pennsylvania society, then, most whites made conscious or unconscious efforts to limit black freedom as much as possible. This simmering resentment made the continued efforts of abolitionists even more important.[4]

At the same time, generations of bondage had left the freed without a foundation to construct their new lives and with few allies to help them. Abolitionists committed to ameliorate the conditions free blacks faced by helping them protect their newly gained freedom, obtain educations, and secure jobs that would allow them to be self-sufficient. This would not be easy, especially as the state's free black population grew and an increasing number of white Pennsylvanians began to want to relocate free and enslaved blacks beyond Pennsylvania's borders. As Pennsylvanians worked out the contours of their postslavery society, leaders explored the possibility of emigration (from the black perspective) or colonization (from the white perspective). The idea of relocating the black population beyond the state's borders, whether to the unsettled western territories, the Caribbean, or Africa, gained popularity throughout the 1820s as Pennsylvania shifted from an antislavery stronghold to an antiblack epicenter by the 1830s.[5]

Philadelphia saw a 48 percent increase in the black population between 1810 and 1830, just as white immigrants, especially from Germany and Ireland, flooded the city. The two migration waves led to job competition that pushed black artisans out of the skilled labor force and forced almost all black Americans to compete with white immigrants for the unskilled and domestic jobs that remained available. As both populations increased, these jobs became increasingly scarce. Jobless and hungry blacks and whites alike committed acts of petty crime to get by, but blacks were more often held accountable. The backlash from the hemisphere's only successful slave rebellion and revolution in Saint-Domingue (which would become Haiti) only added to this tense situation when an influx of white refugees brought graphic and often exaggerated stories about this rebellion with them to Philadelphia.[6]

From the beginning, Quakers felt a sense of responsibility toward the freed. The Visiting Committees reminded Friends of their obligations to those they had freed. Soon after the American Revolution ended, Benezet began to urge abolitionists to reconvene the Society for the Relief of Free Negroes Unlawfully Held in Bondage (the Pennsylvania Abolition Society, or PAS). He discovered two cases in which black men like Cato, who faced being illegally returned to bondage, killed themselves when nobody would help them, and he became determined to prevent that from happening to anyone else. He died on May 3, 1784, leaving fifty pounds in trust to James Starr and Thomas Harrison for the society to use to help blacks illegally detained in slavery and to employ lawyers "and in all other cases afford just relief to those oppressed people."[7]

Encouraged by the cases Benezet brought forward, the PAS resumed formal meetings five months after the Revolutionary War. From 1784 to 1787, the group would help more than one hundred people unlawfully held in bondage regain their freedom with the help of lawyers like William Lewis, who donated his service to the cause. During this second phase of the society's work, it focused mostly on aiding people who had been freed by the abolition law but "who were still being held enslaved because of their own ignorance of the law or their inability to seek relief without outside help."[8]

In late April 1787, the PAS reorganized again, created another constitution, and elected Benjamin Franklin as president. The reconstituted "Pennsylvania Society for Promoting the Abolition of Slavery, the Relief of Free Negroes Unlawfully Held in Bondage, and for Improving the Condition of the Colored Race" and its regional auxiliaries, such as the Washington County Abolition Society in western Pennsylvania, worked to protect the abolition law and see it upheld. In fighting to protect the law, they became increasingly aware of its flaws and recommended a number of changes, including provisions to prevent separating families by more than ten miles, punishment for those who kidnapped free blacks, and measures to make it more difficult to cheat by sending children out of state before they could earn their freedom and sending pregnant women out of state to give birth so that their children would not be born free under the law. They also suggested making it illegal to fit out slave ships in Pennsylvania ports.[9]

The state legislature responded on March 29, 1788, by passing "An Act to Explain and Amend" the 1780 act, which pointed out that the 1780 law provided for the eventual end of slavery in Pennsylvania, but that the end would be a long time coming, with most enslaved Pennsylvanians becoming free only after a life of arduous work. Those born after the law passed remained bound to their enslavers until they were twenty-eight years old. If they had children while they were under this term slavery, those children could be held in bondage until they turned twenty-eight. The same held for future generations, creating the potential for term slavery for many years. Those who gained freedom did so in the later years of their lives and then spent most of their energy trying to gain their children's freedom. Abolitionist lawyers were able to use the courts to exploit technicalities and gain freedom for enslaved people before their terms expired or if their term had been held.[10]

Further attempts of Quakers and PAS members to push for immediate emancipation through either the legislative branch or the judicial branch were continually thwarted. In the 1795 case of *Negro Flora v. Joseph Graisberry*, these abolitionists argued that the state constitution had ended slavery, declaring that all people were born free and independent, with the right to life and liberty. The state supreme court ruled that slavery had legally existed before the 1790 constitution and had not been abolished by it. When this case failed, abolitionists sought to destroy slavery by legal enactment, unsuccessfully petitioning the state senate for complete abolition in 1793. They fought continuously against the provision of the 1780 law that allowed masters to bring slaves to Pennsylvania and keep them there for up to six months, and in 1799 they sent a memorial to legislators, expressing their "deep concern" at the continued keeping of enslaved people in the state. They followed this with yearly petitions to the legislature. Their efforts sometimes resulted in bills being brought forward, but each bill faced ultimate failure. By 1821, it was widely understood that nothing would be done by the legislative or judicial branch to support immediate emancipation.[11]

A United Front

Black leaders who worked independently and with the PAS faced an uphill battle in what historian Gary Nash describes as "an atmosphere of growing Negrophobia in the early nineteenth century." Despite the racial tension, black leaders managed to create a vibrant community and build institutions that took care of more vulnerable members. One of the most important of these institutions was the Free African Society, which was founded in Philadelphia by Richard Allen, Absalom Jones, and William Gray in 1787 and gained the support of white Quakers and PAS members. Through such connections, the Free African Society worked hand in hand with the PAS and the Philadelphia Yearly Meeting to protect and uplift the black community.[12]

Philadelphia black leaders also established two independent churches that served crucial roles in the development of black Philadelphia—the African Episcopal Church of St. Thomas, founded by Absalom Jones in 1792, and Mother Bethel African Methodist Episcopal Church, founded by Richard Allen in 1794. According to Nicholas Wood, these churches served as "sites of activism" that "were especially important for integrating former slaves into the community." According to historian Emma Lapsansky-Werner, the black churches, schools, and antislavery societies served a dual role in that "they cemented the community life of black residents," and "helped to attract hopeful or desperate newcomers to this, the closest big city to the slave South."[13]

Another leader in this generation was James Forten, a Revolutionary War hero who was born free in 1766, served aboard an American privateer in the war, refused to relinquish his U.S. loyalty upon capture by the British in that war, and returned to Philadelphia to prosper as a sailmaker. He became one of the wealthiest men in the state. Like Forten, leaders of this generation worked hard and looked after less fortunate members of the black community, yet they remained relegated to "an ambiguous middle ground between slavery and freedom." Even their heroic actions during the yellow fever outbreak of 1793, during which they worked endlessly to save both black and white lives, only earned them qualified praise from a limited number of whites. Elite and wealthy black families struggled to protect their own material and social gains while also trying to help the working classes who, in historian Philip Lapsansky's words, "lived unseen lives, . . . always only one misstep away from tragedies." The churches, schools, mutual aid societies, literary societies, and political action groups they created served as what he calls a "nucleus of the black abolitionist movement" that allowed leaders to sharpen their skills in community leadership as they fought for abolition and civil rights.[14]

These black leaders worked closely with their white allies in the PAS to reconstruct Pennsylvania society as the free black population grew in the wake of the abolition law. The PAS wrote a "Plan for Improving the Condition of the Free Blacks" in 1789, and in 1790 they created four standing committees to oversee the project. The Committee of Inspection oversaw the morals and conduct of the freed and tried to protect them from unscrupulous whites, while the Committee of Guardians supervised a system of apprenticeship meant to help freedpersons obtain workforce skills. The Committee of Education operated schools and maintained vital records, and the Committee of Employ helped freedpeople find jobs, even if it meant pushing them into indentures. This patriarchal stance was born of class, rather than racial, bias and was shared by black and white leaders alike. Collectively, these committees set forth the reconstruction agenda of the late 1700s and early 1800s.[15]

Together, the PAS and black leaders provided important services to the growing black community. They hired lawyers to consult on manumission cases and keep people informed of their rights. They also fought to keep white immigrants from bringing enslaved workers into the state. Finally, they worked together to protect their black neighbors from kidnapping. Under the Fugitive Slave Law of 1793, all a white person had to do to claim legal ownership of a black person was to swear in court that this person was his or her slave. The PAS protested this law to no avail. In 1799, a group of Philadelphia blacks sent a petition to Congress asking them to do something about kidnapping, arguing that the only sure way to end kidnapping would be to remove the temptation by outlawing slavery altogether.[16]

The most lasting element of this reconstruction agenda involved education, and the Committee of Education was perhaps the strongest of the committees. This group shared Benezet's belief that education would be essential in preparing the freed for productive citizenship in the republic. They hoped that by educating free blacks they could prove to whites that freedpersons could be valuable members of society. They worked with the Free African Society to survey the needs of the black community, and, learning that black families considered education a priority, they began working to create schools for black children. The first sessions of these schools were held at night in the buildings that housed Quaker school sessions for whites during the day. By January of 1793, they had purchased land to build a school specifically for black students and hired a black female teacher. In 1799, Absalom Jones volunteered to teach for them if the PAS would open a school in South Philadelphia, and that same year the PAS began subsidizing schools run by Jones and other black educators. By the end of that year, the PAS was funding the Cherry Street School, Jones's school, and one operated by Amos White, but they then decided to centralize their education operation in a tuition-based school taught by a white teacher they deemed more qualified. They added a school for girls in 1801. At the same time, blacks began operating their own schools. In 1812, the PAS erected a new building, which they named Clarkson Hall in honor of British abolitionist Thomas Clarkson. It housed a boys' school, a girls' school, night schools, a First Day school, a high school, and the PAS headquarters.[17]

While the Committee on Education worked to build and operate schools, the Committee of Employ began working with black leaders in 1789 to help place freedpeople in jobs. The Committee of Guardians had a similar function, though it focused specifically on improving employment opportunities for younger people. Both committees failed by 1810. The problem seems to have been that freedpersons did not seek the help of these committees, choosing instead to work within their own communities and networks to find jobs of their choosing. Even so, the PAS continued to try to find jobs for black men and in 1816 established a Committee of Apprenticeship to help find positions for children whose parents sought their assistance. Again, however, few black parents felt compelled to seek their aid, so they discontinued the committee in 1817.[18]

Fissures Develop

The failure of these committees illustrates the hesitance black Americans felt to defer to whites for help in finding employment. This should come as no surprise, since whites had been keeping blacks enslaved and, no matter their intentions, could not safely be trusted with such matters, at least in the minds of those who were just emerging from captivity and exploitation. Also, the PAS, whether intentionally or not, worsened conditions for blacks seeking employment. Opportunities in the North were even more limited than in the South for free black workers at this time, and the PAS was content to find any kinds of jobs that it could for them. The abolitionists continued to see that the structure of American society excluded black Americans and robbed them of incentives, yet unwittingly perpetuated the relegation of blacks to the lowest rungs of society by encouraging them to take low-paying jobs rather than seek better opportunities.[19]

A similar disconnect occurred when black leaders from the Free African Society and the African Episcopal Church of St. Thomas worked alongside the PAS on the "moral improvement" part of their reconstruction agenda. Here again they shared good intentions, hoping to advance the status of free blacks by helping them to fit into society, but again they failed. In 1789, the PAS created a Committee of Inspection, which met with members of the Free African Society to develop a general plan for improving the condition of freedpeople. Neither of these groups seemed to realize, however, how condescending part of their mission appeared. It might be helpful to offer someone "protection from wrongs," but it was an entirely different matter to take on the task of supervising another person's "morals" and "general conduct." This is another instance in which class biases, rather than racial biases, created a gulf between those who were trying to build a new life in freedom and those who wanted to help but failed to see beyond their own biases and paternalistic outlook to truly understand the conditions people were facing. Not surprisingly, this committee also failed to appeal to the very people it hoped to assist.[20]

By 1799, black and white cooperation in the reconstruction agenda was beginning to weaken. At this point, black leaders found themselves at odds with the PAS and offered a plan of their own to the state legislature. Realizing that emancipation was going no further in the state, and that in many ways their white allies were out of touch with reality if they believed that good behavior on the part of blacks would lead to white respect, much less full emancipation, they offered the legislature a plan to tax free blacks to help fund compensated emancipation for those still in bondage. Though the plan would have freed all remaining slaves in Pennsylvania, the PAS opposed it because such a plan served to acknowledge the legitimacy of bondage and to reward slaveholders. This stance was at odds with the practice of some individual Quakers who had been buying people to free them, and the disagreement over this tactic would continue until the Civil War. The PAS wanted to hold out for the day they could get slavery declared unconstitutional, but those who had family in bondage were less likely to believe that would ever happen. Unfortunately, however, the plan backfired as whites in Chester and Delaware Counties built on the original premise to argue for special taxes on free blacks to support indigent blacks.[21]

Growing Backlash

Pessimism spread to white abolitionists as it became increasingly clear that Pennsylvania society would not be reconstructed in a way that would offer equal opportunities for black Americans. Indeed, abolitionist success led to backlash as soon as the emancipation law passed. In 1790, the PAS submitted to the first U.S. Congress a petition calling for national abolition, leading whites across the country to label them radicals. From the beginning they were accused of fostering racial mixing, endangering the new nation by causing sectional tensions, and encouraging free blacks to seek asylum in the state. Adding to this existing tension, the acquisition of western lands through the Louisiana Purchase and the corresponding heated debates over the spread of slavery into those territories left the abolitionists even less popular. By 1809, a strong backlash was building against Pennsylvania abolitionists, leading the PAS to exhibit increasing caution in its efforts and to regret the influx of black immigrants to Pennsylvania.[22]

Black leaders also came to feel threatened by the new arrivals. In the 1790s, the relatively small size of the black population bred familiarity, but as the community grew, neighbors became strangers. As the black middle class began to form in the early nineteenth century, members of that class began to worry that the presence and behavior of the newcomers would stigmatize all blacks, including themselves. This concern was supported by a rise in the proportion of black inmates in Walnut Street Prison, most of whom had come from other states and countries. Between 1793 and 1800, the number of blacks in Philadelphia prosecuted for property crimes tripled. Of course, as in the twenty-first century, prosecution and imprisonment rates reflected white perceptions of the black community more than it reflected the rate of black criminal activity. While some blacks distanced themselves from newcomers because they did not want to be assumed to be part of the criminal element, most received newcomers with respect and offered assistance despite any concerns they had.[23]

As the black population grew, more whites came to fear the idea of black retribution for past wrongs. A series of arson attempts by enraged blacks in York in 1803 led the governor to call in the militia, adding to this fear. The influx of white Haitian refugees who brought their enslaved people as well as graphic tales of black brutality made the situation even worse. The climate of fear escalated to the point that the mayor of Lancaster implemented a registration system that required all blacks to announce themselves or forfeit their right to stay in the borough in 1820. Finally, Pennsylvania's proximity to states that maintained slavery led residents to consider the imminent danger of revolts.[24]

Though whites made much of their fear of the growing black population, blacks were more likely to be legally and physically targeted by whites. Whites began to propose laws to restrict black mobility, impose taxes on free blacks, and enable town governments to sell the labor of blacks convicted of crimes. The first attempts to prevent black migration into the state came as early as 1798, when Governor Thomas Mifflin prohibited the landing of additional French blacks from Saint-Domingue, but this was a specific and limited attempt that ultimately failed. A more sustained and widely threatening exclusion campaign began in 1805 with the proposal of the first in a series of bills to either prevent black migration or tax African American householders to support indigents.

Between 1805 and 1807, three such bills passed one branch of the legislature or another, though none ultimately passed into law. In 1813, Congressman Jacob Mitchell, a Philadelphia Republican merchant, offered a bill that would have required every black resident to register or face enslavement or imprisonment, stipulated that black criminals be sold and the revenue used to pay restitution to victims, and taxed black householders to support black indigents. Unlike previous bills, this one had the support of Philadelphia's mayor and aldermen. The black community united in protest, with James Forten issuing "Letters from a Man of Colour," which employed the rhetoric of the American Revolution, a war in which he had fought, to argue against the bill and on behalf of the black community. The PAS joined in the resistance, and the bill failed, but efforts through 1814 encouraged the development of racial segregation during public events, such as Fourth of July celebrations, and in public accommodations.[25]

Even as they complained about poor blacks taking up public resources, whites targeted prosperous blacks in verbal and physical altercations, revealing their resentment of black achievement and success. Despite efforts to deny black Pennsylvanians gainful employment and other opportunities, they found ways to support themselves, some quite well. At the bottom of the social and economic ladder were those who toiled for the meager wages they could obtain through manual labor in the cities and the countryside. These jobs included work in the maritime field as well as in iron and other industries, including tanning, carpentry, and blacksmithing. In addition to domestic service in white households, women found outwork as seamstresses and laundresses. Not all blacks ended up in manual labor, however, and the black community included business owners who enjoyed varying degrees of success. Some, such as the women known for selling pepper pot stew in Philadelphia, made a living as pushcart vendors. Other men and women owned and operated taverns, hotels, and boarding houses. Cyrus Bustill made a name for himself as a noted baker in Philadelphia, and Rachel Lloyd operated a restaurant in Walnut Street Theater from 1808 to 1850. Many black men in the cities found a great deal of success in the catering and barbering fields.[26]

Black communities throughout Pennsylvania developed their own churches, schools, benevolent organizations, and intellectual societies. Philadelphia was home to the first independent black churches and the Free African Society. Pittsburgh blacks, numbering 2,500 by 1837, founded their own African Methodist Episcopal (AME) church, which boasted 250 members and a successful Sunday school with a black teacher. Pittsburgh also had a temperance society, four benevolent societies, the Theban Literary Society, and a moral reform society. Philadelphia's intellectual organizations included the Philadelphia Library Company and Debating Society and the Banneker Institute. By the mid-1830s, black women in Pennsylvania had at least two literary societies of their own. Black schools included the Institute for Colored Youth in Philadelphia and Avery College in Pittsburgh. Through these organizations, the black community policed itself and used the concept of self-help to prove their worthiness for citizenship. Black women especially used mutual aid societies and church tribunals to maintain order and civility in their communities and "protect the image of free black Philadelphia."[27] Through their hard work, many blacks achieved more success than whites wanted to allow.

Blacks who dared to live according to their economic means and enjoy finery such as nice clothing and carriages faced the threat of being attacked by jealous whites. By 1820, tensions between blacks and whites, particularly white immigrants, were leading to race riots and attacks on black neighborhoods in cities like Philadelphia, Carlisle, and others.[28] This atmosphere led both blacks and whites to consider the merits of racial separation.

The Appeal of Resettlement

Black Americans had been considering resettlement to Africa since their forced arrival to the New World, but as the generations became further removed from their ancestral land, most free blacks came to focus on making a life for themselves in the United States. After all, they would argue, their work and that of their ancestors had built the new nation. By the late 1780s, however, some black leaders had come to consider the possibility that equality would be impossible in the United States and to explore the idea of emigrating to Africa. British philanthropists and the English government were in the process of working together to create and sponsor the African settlement of Sierra Leone for black expatriates, and the idea gained some consideration in the United States.

Black American sea captain Paul Cuffe of Massachusetts reached out to Richard Allen, Absalom Jones, and James Forten to seek their support in an emigration scheme to take American blacks to Sierra Leone. Allen was initially favorable to the plan, having come to believe that future generations would likely be unable to manage to find the success his generation had. He also hoped, as a bishop in the AME Church, that African settlement would spread his religious mission to Africa. This idea was thwarted, however, when the black community rejected colonization out of hand, suspicious of white leadership of the enterprise and fearful that it would serve simply as a prelude to forced removal. Eventually black leaders took their cue and presented an anticolonization pamphlet to their white antislavery allies. Even so, Forten and Allen, among others, continued to consider the merits of emigration to Haiti, and many black Americans would settle, at least temporarily, in Africa, Haiti, or other locations of black resettlement.[29]

As black Americans were rejecting resettlement, growing numbers of white Americans were embracing it. Benezet's reparation plan was in some ways a resettlement plan, since it would have provided land beyond the Allegheny Mountains to blacks. PAS member Benjamin Rush learned of Benezet's plan in the late 1790s and hoped to implement something similar to give blacks an opportunity to "obtain employment . . . more congenial to their knowledge and former habits." He offered to donate 5,200 acres of land in Bedford County to create a settlement and name it after Benezet. Both plans were intended to give blacks land in settlements where they could prosper independently, but neither was intended to remove blacks from white society. Both Thomas Paine and Philadelphia Quaker John Parrish advocated resettling free blacks on Louisiana Purchase lands on homesteads granted by the federal government. Parrish claimed that such a settlement would encourage southerners to emancipate their captives. Abolitionist Thomas Branagan advocated a similar scheme of sending blacks into the western territories of North America. This idea gained popularity among many whites of the Revolutionary generation and is often discussed by historians as the concept of "diffusion."[30]

The PAS even grappled with the idea of resettlement. To begin with, slaveholders in states that prohibited emancipation or coupled it with the requirement that blacks leave once freed had been reaching out to the PAS since the 1780s for help in resettling their freedpeople. Given the hostility around them, the PAS found it increasingly difficult to accept such refugees. PAS members Roberts Vaux and Thomas P. Cope wrote a petition asking the government to ban the domestic slave trade and to consider setting aside federal territory in the West for resettlement of enslaved people whose owners would free them but could not do so because of existing state laws. In a case such as this, in which resettlement fostered emancipation, the abolitionists were supportive, but they would eventually reject colonization as a proslavery endeavor once a new group, the American Colonization Society (ACS), formed under the leadership of a number of slaveholders along with a handful of philanthropists in 1817.[31]

Whether abolitionists supported colonization or not, a significant portion of Pennsylvania's white population did by the late 1820s. Northern border states like Pennsylvania played an important role in the growth and development of the colonization movement because of their geographic position, and the ACS hoped especially to gain support in Pennsylvania because of its reputation as an antislavery stronghold. The society was founded by a mixed group of people with complex motives, some of whom wanted to remove free blacks and strengthen the institution of slavery and others who wanted to encourage manumissions by giving slaveholders an outlet to send away those they freed. Pennsylvanians who chose to support the endeavor did so for many reasons. To those who supported it for selfish and racist reasons, colonization offered relief from the growing black population. Others supported it for more altruistic reasons, truly believing that it would lead slaveholders who otherwise would not do so to free the human beings they held captive. By 1830, Pennsylvania was home to one of the strongest ACS state auxiliaries, the Pennsylvania Colonization Society (PCS). Its leading members included philanthropist Elliott Cresson, who supported the cause as an antislavery endeavor, and Mathew Carey, who supported it out of a nationalist desire to develop the United States as an industrial, rather than an agrarian, nation and as a means of diffusing a potentially dangerous population.[32]

Growth of Segregation and Violent Resistance to Black Freedom

Reconstruction failed in Pennsylvania, as it did in every other state in the United States at one point or another. Postemancipation optimism gave way to pessimism by 1830, as enslavement was replaced by segregation and racial oppression. Columbia County offers a case study through which to view this process. Quakers there had been known for creating safe houses to help fugitive slaves escape from the South, but racial and class divisions deepened in the postemancipation years. The first Quaker settlers to Wright's Ferry, the future site of Columbia County, brought enslaved workers with them in 1726. By 1788, German and Scots Irish settlers began to outnumber English Quakers, and by 1801 the settlement contained ten free blacks and no enslaved people. In 1819, a Virginia slaveholder freed fifty-six people, and the town founders provided land for a settlement for them, creating the neighborhood of Tow Hill. In 1821, when another Virginia slaveholder manumitted one hundred enslaved people, many of them augmented the population of Tow Hill. The Columbia Abolition Society, founded by English Quakers in 1818, took on the task of protecting the freedpersons from whites, who noticed the growing black population and sought to profit by kidnapping people and selling them, under the guise that they were returning slaves to their masters.[33]

By 1820, out of a total population of 1,092, there were 64 enslaved and 288 free blacks, most of whom had migrated from Maryland and upper Virginia. At this point, Columbia, though a small city, resembled Philadelphia in it that it included a large percentage of free blacks living near whites and an emergent black middle class that drew the jealousy of white workers. Economic opportunities allowed blacks like Stephen Smith to carve out a niche in the city. Smith, who had been born into term slavery in 1795 to a mother who had been registered as a slave in Lancaster County, managed to obtain start-up money through loans from white merchants and opened his own lumber business in 1816. His business became profitable, and he was able to invest heavily in Columbia real estate, irritating poor and working-class whites in the city. By 1833, he was worth the significant sum of $6,500 and was, at one point, the "largest stakeholder in the Columbia Bank." He was not the only successful black Columbian, as thirty-six other black property owners collectively owned $8,460 in real estate.

In late 1830, for a variety of reasons, many of the original members of the Columbia Abolition Society created a new group, the Columbia Auxiliary Colonization Society. Prominent blacks denounced this society and "resolved to oppose all attempts at colonization in Liberia," but the society grew in popularity among whites, spurred by the racial tensions that swept the northeast in 1834, a year in which Columbia saw its own outbreak in racial violence when lower-class whites targeted black property owners in Tow Hill, including Smith. The violence here, as would be the case in many other U.S. cities in the wake of regional emancipation, grew partly out of rumors of marriage between a white woman and a black man. The unrest eventually led to a threat on Smith's life, but local white leader William Wright used the local newspaper as a mouthpiece to make it clear that "any attack on Smith" would be an "attack upon their own financial interests in Smith's business," so he was spared, though the white population remained divided in their racial sentiments.[34] The events in Columbia mirrored those throughout the state as whites came to terms with black freedom and blacks fought to defend their place in Pennsylvania society.

———

BY THE 1830S, slavery had largely disappeared from Pennsylvania and the region, though because of the gradual terms of abolition, it remained legal in Pennsylvania until 1865. Over the next several decades, Philadelphia's status as a port city and its border with slaveholding states continued to attract fugitive slaves from the South and to aggravate whites who resented black neighbors, whether they were poor or wealthy. While the first emancipation changed the demographics of the mid-Atlantic by replacing enslaved with freed blacks, real change would not come for black Pennsylvanians until the early twentieth century, and even that change remained limited in scope.[35]

Because the North was undergoing its reconstruction while slavery grew and expanded in the South, the North was able to create its own version of what would later be called Jim Crow segregation in the post–Civil War South, but to do so while hiding behind what was going on below the Mason-Dixon Line. In a world where somewhere else still sanctioned human bondage, having given up that institution provided a moral high ground that allowed northerners to rest on their laurels and stop short of truly reconstructing their own society on the basis of equality. They could focus on what was going on in the South and ignore what was happening around them as black Americans were being excluded, targeted, and attacked.

The early abolitionists realized this and pushed beyond state boundaries to solve this problem. While historians have sometimes described them as more conservative than the abolitionists of the 1830s, recent works are reminding us that they were the radicals of their day. They were called fanatics and accused of jeopardizing the new nation's stability by encouraging sectional discord. Yet they persisted, and despite the failures of reconstruction around them, they pushed to spread freedom beyond Pennsylvania and the mid-Atlantic. Before we turn to the rise of immediate abolition in the 1830s, we must understand the story of these early abolitionists and their role in maintaining the momentum of the antislavery movement.

6

ABOLITION BEYOND PENNSYLVANIA

CHARITY KNEW they would be coming for her soon. It had been a while since she and Harriet fled to Philadelphia to escape the abuse. When they left, it was unclear how long they would stay. Now that they had been away for almost six months, Harriet would have the luxury of continuing her sanctuary in the city, while Charity faced being returned to bondage in the household of their abuser. The man they had escaped from, Charles Carroll Jr., was the son of one of the wealthiest men in the United States. His father, Charles Carroll of Carrollton, had signed the Declaration of Independence and then served as a U.S. senator. He continued to hold ten thousand acres of property and approximately a thousand human beings in Maryland.

Charles Jr. benefitted from his father's wealth in the way that most sons of planters did. Having grown up in a household where wealth depended on the forced labor of others, he had no qualms about claiming to own human beings, including Charity. Apparently, neither did his wife, Harriet. She was the daughter of one of Pennsylvania's largest slaveholders, Benjamin Chew, another major political figure in the mid-Atlantic. When the young couple married, the elder Carroll gave them an estate in Maryland named Home-wood, where they could create a family of their own, but the loss of two children and his own declining health led Charles Jr. to turn to alcohol. He then began to abuse the people he held control over in one way or another—his wife, his children, and those he kept in bondage. Aware of the abuse, the Chews and the Carrolls agreed that Harriet and the children must leave

Homewood. When she left for her parents' home in Philadelphia, Harriet took Charity with her.[1]

As their time in Philadelphia neared six months, both Harriet and Charity realized that Charity's continued presence in Pennsylvania would lead to her freedom under the 1780 abolition law. While in Pennsylvania, Charity had managed to make a life for herself, apparently even finding a partner of her own in the city. Harriet, however, was unwilling to challenge her husband's ownership of Charity and turned to her brother, Benjamin Chew Jr., to arrange Charity's return. As Chew negotiated with the Carroll family, Charity suffered serious injuries in an accident while working. A doctor diagnosed her injuries severe enough to make travel unsafe. She remained unable to travel well beyond the six-month residence period allowed by the abolition law.[2]

Once the six-month period expired, two members of the Pennsylvania Abolition Society (PAS) became involved, but they offered different interpretations of Charity's case. Charity's husband reached out to Judge William Lewis, one of the main authors of the gradual abolition act, for his advice and assistance. Based on what he learned from the couple, Lewis offered them a written opinion in which he declared Charity free by Pennsylvania law and said that she could not be taken back to Maryland. Unsatisfied with Lewis's assessment, Benjamin Chew reached out to William Rawle, another lawyer affiliated with the PAS. According to Rawle, the master had not kept Charity in Pennsylvania, the accident had. Since the master did not cause the accident, he was not "answerable" for it. Thus, Rawle concluded that Charity had not gained her freedom. As the Chews and Carrolls tried to sort it out, William Lewis sent notice to Harriet that he had advised Charity's husband "to take her to himself," and that if Mr. Carroll came to claim her in a legal manner to "be forthcoming when properly called for." With that, Charity apparently gained her freedom on Christmas Eve of 1814.[3]

Nobody knows for sure if the accident was indeed an accident or a ruse. What is clear is that Charity knew the law, and her husband knew to turn to the PAS for guidance and assistance. Though they trusted Lewis and some of his associates, they also realized that some, like Rawle, were more conservative in their interpretation of the law, so they knew to remain guarded. Ultimately, Charity took her fate into her own hands and disappeared.[4]

The Charity Castle case showcases the complexities of the early antislavery movement in Pennsylvania. The letters between the slaveholders illustrate the ways in which they tried to protect their interests. In the face of coordinated resistance, however, they sometimes found it hard to win against determined blacks. The presence of white allies such as the more activist PAS members complicated matters even further. The case also shows that enslaved and free blacks knew about the law and its loopholes and were willing to use them to their advantage whenever they could. They maintained hope that if they fought the system with determination they could wear it down eventually. Further, the story shows that black Americans trusted their white allies when they could but realized they had to exercise caution and not trust anyone too much. Just as importantly, the case points to the tensions that resulted when slave states and free states shared borders. Finally, Charity's case illustrates the complexity of the period that is often called the "gradual" abolition era. It shows that even among abolitionists a variety of opinions and interpretations competed in the debate over how best to end slavery and rebuild society. While some were more conservative, early radicals adhered to a human rights vision of equality and universal liberty.[5]

Spreading Abolition beyond Pennsylvania

The efforts of abolitionist Quakers spread beyond the boundaries of Pennsylvania even before the American Revolution. In 1755, North Carolina Quakers approved the Philadelphia Yearly Meeting's 1754 *Epistle of Caution and Advice, Concerning the Buying and Keeping of Slaves*, and in 1757 they established the North Carolina Standing Committee. That committee was modeled after the Pennsylvania Meeting for Sufferings, the group that oversaw much of the antislavery work. The North Carolina Yearly Meeting did not completely fall in line when the Philadelphia Yearly Meeting forbade slave trading, but it at least called on members to treat enslaved people well and establish worship meetings for them. In addition to North Carolina, antislavery Quakers made inroads into Delaware, Maryland, northern Virginia, and New Jersey, creating what historian Nicholas Wood described as "a national network of abolitionists," with members who "functioned as a national antislavery lobby." The Philadelphia Yearly Meeting's Meeting for Sufferings fostered the creation of state abolition societies throughout the mid-Atlantic and upper South in the 1780s. Along with these allies, it repeatedly petitioned neighboring state governments and the federal government to pass antislavery legislation throughout the 1790s. Quakers often dominated the societies, but they made sure to infuse them with secular and interdenominational elements that allowed them to connect antislavery efforts to the American Revolution and to argue that ending slavery was a national cause.[6]

The state societies served three main functions. First, they assisted black Americans, whether enslaved or free, with legal cases, employment, and education. Second, they lobbied state lawmakers to pass or strengthen laws that forbade owning and trading in human beings. Finally, they lobbied at the federal level to convince the national government to end slave trading and promote gradual emancipation. Warner Mifflin epitomized the activist Quaker lobbyist, traveling from state to state to promote antislavery action. According to his biographer, he introduced "methods of reaching those with power that became the hallmark of modern politicking." While more conservative abolitionists worked to conciliate their southern neighbors, Mifflin's efforts gained him a reputation among southerners as "a menace to the new republic" and "the most dangerous man in America." Southerners "detested his repeated exercise of the right of petition" against the slave trade and slavery, and they "hated his argument that . . . God would punish Americans for 'national sins.'" He angered slaveholders by leading a group of Quakers in approaching the first national Congress to lobby against human bondage, and, unlike many of his generation, he took an unapologetic stance, working undauntedly as a "fearless figure, willing to wage war against the evil of slavery with an intensity that historians usually associate with the militant abolitionism of the antebellum decades."[7]

One of the best examples of Pennsylvania abolitionists' activism beyond state lines and lobbying of the federal government involved refugees from North Carolina. The saga began when North Carolina Quakers followed the Philadelphia Yearly Meeting's directive to free adults held in slavery or face disownment. Torn between their faith, which dictated they free their bondspeople, or the laws of their state, which forbade emancipation, North Carolina Quakers decided to liberate those they had held in slavery and to help them fight re-enslavement by the state by recording manumissions and hiring lawyers for them. Many of the freed left North Carolina in order to avoid re-enslavement, and many of them headed to Philadelphia. Once they arrived, they found black and white allies among the city's antislavery community and, along with their help, became the first black Americans to petition Congress. The petition was presented to Congress in January of 1797 by a delegation that included four black Americans and white Quakers Mifflin and John Parrish. It failed because of the argument that Congress held no jurisdiction over state laws, but the work behind it illustrates the activism and racial cooperation that was central to the antislavery movement throughout the struggle. Members of the group worked together to send a second petition to Congress in 1799, but it also failed. According to Wood, however, the petition campaigns did result in affirmation of the right of black Americans to petition Congress. The 1799 effort also led to the passage of the Slave Trade Act of 1800, which forbade U.S. citizens from importing enslaved people into the United States. Most importantly, the overall effort "antici-pated tactics that scholars still associate with the second wave of abolitionism in the 1830s."[8]

Immediately after the U.S. Constitution went into effect, southerners began to argue that states' rights limited the influence of the national govern-ment, particularly regarding slavery, but activist abolitionists of this genera-tion worked around this argument by seeking to expand the notion of federal jurisdiction. They focused primarily on the slave trade and the status of fed-eral territories, but they also petitioned for general abolition. Jurisdiction over slavery and the slave trade had not been unequivocally established, and they worked to convince Congress to consider human rights over property rights. They were encouraged by the fact that leaders in the upper South like Thomas Jefferson supported gradual emancipation and that control over slavery and the slave trade was still being negotiated. Gary Nash describes this generation as "experienced lobbyists and men fiercely intent on trying to save the nation from the seeds of self-destruction that continued to germinate with slave dealing and slaveholding."[9]

In addition to their efforts for North Carolina blacks, Revolutionary-era abolitionists appealed to the leaders of Virginia, Delaware, Maryland, and New Jersey. Just after the Battle of Yorktown, John Parrish and Warner Miff-lin set out for Richmond to try to push a manumission bill through the Gen-eral Assembly in Virginia. They presented their bill and were allowed to watch the debate over it. After it was sent to committee, they were able to discuss it with individual committee members, seeking them out in legislative cham-bers, the streets, and even in their boarding houses. The effort paid off when a manumission bill was passed in June of 1782. In Delaware they turned to John Dickinson to draft a gradual abolition law in 1785. That bill failed, but Delaware did pass a law in 1787 that eliminated the personal security bond for healthy people manumitted between the ages of eighteen and thirty-five, criminalized the sale of enslaved and indentured blacks to the lower South and West Indies unless signed off on by three justices of the peace, freed any person brought into the state as a slave, and imposed a hundred-pound fine for kid-napping free blacks and sending them South. The bill had serious limitations, but it was, according to Nash, "enough to worry slaveowners and traffickers." It did give enslaved people the right to sue, and many began seeking Mifflin out for legal counsel. As he met with them, he also worked with whites in the state to form the Delaware Society for Promoting the Abolition of Slavery in Dover. This nondenominational group recruited the state's governor to serve as its president and enlisted Revolutionary War heroes to fill leading offices while Quakers worked in the background to deal with the legal cases. Another group in Wilmington, the Delaware Society for the Gradual Abolition of Slavery, was led more conspicuously by Quakers. The activists also labored in New Jersey and Maryland, gaining abolition in the former in 1804, but failing in the latter.[10]

Once abolitionists built antislavery societies along the Eastern Seaboard, they began to bring them together to work in a more organized manner, and they formalized this relationship in 1794 by creating the American Convention of Abolition Societies. The Pennsylvania Abolition Society was clearly the dominant force in this organization, but the New York Manumission Society (NYMS) was also highly active. These two groups sent delegates to every one of the twenty-five conventions that met from 1794 to 1829, all but four of which assembled in Philadelphia. Eleven states and the District of Columbia participated in at least one meeting, with the New Jersey and Delaware societies being the second most active. The last convention assembled in 1829 in Washington, DC, and the PAS and NYMS met one final time in 1837 to dissolve the group's assets and determine what to do with its archives, which can still be found with the PAS Papers at the Historical Society of Pennsylvania. Like the PAS, the American Convention contained more cautious as well as more activist members who worked side by side. According to one historian, they balanced optimism that slaveholders could eventually be won over to the cause of human freedom with a more "pessimistic realism" that relied on mass political pressure on the federal government to force states to do the right thing. Through this organization, the various abolition societies found support and solidarity among allies as they fought the slave trade and worked to protect free blacks throughout the United States.[11]

Abolitionists of this generation carried on the battle against the international slave trade, using their lobbying and petitioning skills to try to convince Congress to stop the importation of human cargoes. The American Revolution had halted the international trade, and they hoped to prevent its postwar resumption, so the Philadelphia Yearly Meeting petitioned Congress to this end. Congress first dashed abolitionists' hopes by refusing to prohibit human trafficking at the national level, but it did pass the 1794 Foreign Slave Trade Act, the first federal law to curb the slave trade. It followed with additional legislation in 1800 and 1807. The House, however, gave in to the demands of slaveholders by allowing for humans illegally brought in as slaves to be confiscated and disposed of by the state in which they landed. This gave the states the legal right to sell them into slavery, thus weakening the overall effect of the law. The PAS and their allies in the American Convention fought this development, and Congress passed a new law in 1819 providing that these contraband humans, known as "recaptives," be returned to Africa. Unfortunately, they were returned to the U.S. settlement in Africa, rather than to their place of origin. This law, in effect, established what would become the nation of Liberia. It had cross-sectional support for its potential in suppressing the Atlantic Slave Trade.[12]

Fighting Kidnappers and the Interstate Slave Trade

Once state and federal legislation banned the Atlantic trade, abolitionists turned their focus to the even more challenging fight against the interstate slave trade. Pennsylvania slave owners had been using this avenue to dispose of enslaved laborers even before the abolition law passed, and Pennsylvania abolitionists realized that as long as slavery remained legal in other states, slaveholders would continue to face the temptation of selling people to southern states, even after it was illegal. Further, as settlement spread south and west into the highly productive area known as the "Deep South," particularly after Eli Whitney's cotton gin provided a new avenue for vast profits, the economic value of enslaved humans grew exponentially. This left slave owners in the mid-Atlantic, even in places such as Delaware where slavery remained legal, tempted to sell their captives to brokers who would then sell them on the internal slave market for vast profits.[13]

Abolitionists fought the internal trade for many reasons, one of which was the fact that it created incentive for kidnappers. Slave hunters profited from chasing down and returning people like Charity who had been legally held in bondage but had managed to escape. These "slave catchers" were working within legal boundaries prescribed by Article IV, Section 14, of the U.S. Constitution's mandate that someone held to "service or labor" in one state be returned to the state from which they escaped, which was upheld by a fugitive law in 1793. Others, however, worked outside the law and kidnapped free blacks, claiming they were escaped slaves. Abolitionists introduced a memorial to the Pennsylvania state legislature in 1811 calling for stricter penalties for those who kidnapped free blacks. The resulting act, which passed the legislature in 1820, imposed fines ranging from $500 to $2,000 and prison sentences ranging from seven to twenty-one years for people convicted of kidnapping free blacks.[14]

This anti-kidnapping law led to a standoff between Pennsylvania and Maryland in the 1820s. Cases of violent resistance to slave hunters at this time led Maryland legislators to accuse Pennsylvanians of encouraging violent resistance to the fugitive slave law. Maryland leaders reached out to the Pennsylvania Assembly to do something about the situation. In response, the PAS wrote to the legislature that the problem resulted not from their legal efforts to defend black Americans, but from the violent actions of slave catchers. If those who hoped to pursue fugitives would work through the courts and use legal means rather than vigilante apprehension tactics such as armed confrontation, there would be no violence involved, the PAS argued. Maryland leaders continued to complain to Pennsylvania lawmakers, and abolitionists continued to push back throughout the 1820s.[15] Though PAS activist members would find and exploit every loophole they could to help the fugitive, their work remained within the bounds of law.

There was a fine line between legal duty to cooperate in fugitive cases and allowing kidnapping, and abolitionists knew it. When the Maryland legislature sent a delegation to Pennsylvania to work out a more effective way to recover fugitives in 1826, black and white abolitionists offered immediate resistance. They argued that the legislation Maryland sought to foist onto Pennsylvania would lead to the kidnapping of free blacks, and Richard Allen traveled to Harrisburg to testify about his personal experience at the hands of a kidnapper who had once tried to claim him as a fugitive. A Pennsylvania Meeting for Sufferings delegation also went to the capitol to lobby for amendments that would put safeguards in the final bill to prevent kidnapping. The result was legislation that included strong protection for Pennsylvanians' legal rights, though the dispute over fugitive slave legislation and its connection to kidnapping would continue as long as slavery remained anywhere in the nation.[16]

The line between slave catcher and kidnapper was frequently blurry, since most fugitive slave cases hinged on unreliable eyewitness testimony as to whether the supposed slave was or was not the person slave catchers claimed. In such a system, it was easy for a slave catcher to seize someone who was not actually a fugitive and "return" him or her to a slave owner for a reward. This could, and did, easily devolve into profiteers hunting down free blacks and selling them into slavery. This problem would become increasingly serious after the 1820s, but abolitionists began resisting kidnappers in the 1790s.[17]

Disputes over slave catching and kidnapping gained broader meaning and wider geographic dimensions as the United States added more and more western territory. At that point, neighbors' quarrels like the one between Pennsylvania and Maryland took on national dimensions as legislators from free and slave states began to fight over whether slavery would spread into each new territory. Abolitionists had lobbied Congress to oppose the territorial expansion of slavery since the 1790s, but the issue gained national prominence during the Missouri Crisis of 1819 to 1821. The American Convention met in 1819 to discuss whether the U.S. government had constitutional power to restrict slavery in new territories that sought entry into the United States.

Arguing that the founders would not have intended for slavery to be allowed to spread and citing the power given to Congress to restrict slavery from new territories, they concluded that the national government did have the power to restrict slavery from Missouri, Arkansas, and other future states. By 1821, the PAS expressed a growing concern that the interests of the free and slave states were generally incompatible. When proslavery forces won the contest over Missouri's status, the abolition movement suffered a serious setback. According to Wood, this fight over the status of slavery in Missouri "exacerbated sectional tensions" to the point of "reducing the potential for antislavery cooperation" and left colonization as "the only form of antislavery action that had any potential for cross-sectional political appeal."[18]

The Pennsylvania Colonization Society

The African recolonization movement in Pennsylvania saw its heyday in the 1820s. The Pennsylvania Colonization Society (PCS) gained most of its support during this period, for two different reasons. On the one hand, abolitionists who wanted to end slavery and protect the welfare of black Americans turned to colonization as they faced increasing disenchantment when the Missouri tensions translated into even more backlash against abolitionists and free blacks in the state. On the other hand, colonization was attractive to people who opposed slavery for political reasons that included racist visions of the United States as a white nation bound for industrial and economic greatness. This latter group developed an ideology that historians refer to as the "American System." Adherents believed that the United States would only reach its full potential if it limited its agricultural dependence and cultivated modern systems of transportation that would support private industry. In this type of society, slavery was an antiquated and inefficient labor system that divided the nation racially, created a permanent lower class and the economic and social tensions that go with it, and held back progress.[19]

Regardless of which side of the colonization divide they were on, most people in Pennsylvania who supported the movement did so out of opposition to slavery. Some hoped to use the Slave Trade Act of 1807 to combat the Atlantic slave trade and choke slavery out by preventing future imports. Many also hoped that this act, by establishing the settlement of Liberia, would provide a base from which black and white Americans could establish churches and schools and spread Christianity throughout Africa. Some hoped that black Americans would find in Liberia a place that was free of the racism and discrimination they faced in the United States. Others, however, just hoped Liberia would provide a place to send black Americans, slave and free, to make more room for white immigrants in the United States. At a time in which the nation was becoming increasingly divided, colonization offered something for almost everyone.

The PCS revived in 1827 after a stagnant beginning earlier in the decade. It then began to raise money and prepare memorials to the state government in hopes of gaining its support for the cause. A number of local and county societies formed by the late 1820s and went to work raising money and support right away. By 1829, they had managed to convince the Pennsylvania legislature to set aside $2,000 to send Pennsylvania blacks to Liberia. By the end of 1830, the American Colonization Society (ACS) had raised almost $4,000 in Pennsylvania and had convinced the PCS to fund and oversee an expedition to take conditionally freed people to Africa. The PCS spent more than $3,200 to send 128 colonists, most of whom had been freed on the condition they leave the United States, to Liberia. At least thirty-one PAS members joined either the ACS or the PCS or contributed money to the effort to send emigrants to the colony.[20] The majority of abolitionists, however, ultimately concluded that colonization had promise if and only if it were voluntary.

Multiple Challenges

The abolition movement faced many challenges throughout the 1820s in addition to the rising popularity of the African colonization movement. For one matter, a popular adherence to states' rights ideology and strict construction of the Constitution left little room for antislavery action in U.S. politics. At the same time, massive waves of poor and working-class immigrants, especially from Ireland, led to more competition among workers and more reason for working-class whites to resent free blacks. Further, a growing sense of anti-abolitionism during the period reflected racism throughout the nation, but it also reveals the widespread belief that antislavery agitation "was more likely to lead to disunion than peaceful emancipation." Finally, the abolition movement faced the loss of some Quaker support at the very moment it most needed all the help it could get to repel these outward forces. This occurred in 1827, when the Society of Friends split over differing perspectives on benevolent activism and participation in non-Quaker reform groups.[21]

Despite these difficulties, abolitionists remained committed to the cause. They focused on fighting against the internal slave trade and the extension of slavery, and they continued to push for improvements in the lives of free blacks. They continued to ask state governments to take incremental measures to end slavery without violating the U.S. Constitution, such as ending slavery in the District of Columbia and the territories and abolishing the interstate slave trade. According to Nash, this generation and their children "kept alive the idea of universal freedom and the vision of a biracial democracy, while inching toward the more radical abolitionism" of the immediatist era. Wood adds that "nationwide emancipation and equal rights may have been out of reach, but black and white activists achieved important victories against slaveholders' efforts to reverse the era's limited antislavery gains." Aware that the Constitution provided major impediments to their work, they remained confident that they could fight the system from within.[22]

Historians have made much of the difference between these "gradualists" and the "immediatists" who emerged in the 1830s, but there was little difference between the groups in Pennsylvania. Regardless of which generation they fit into, Pennsylvania abolitionists harbored different and often conflicting views over antislavery tactics. From the early years of Benjamin Lay and John Woolman to the postwar generation of William Rawle and William Lewis and beyond, abolitionists in Pennsylvania argued among themselves over how best to end slavery. Some chose more radical or aggressive tactics like Lay's theatrics or Warner Mifflin's incessant lobbying, while others took more cautious approaches. What they all shared, however, was the desire to end slavery as quickly as they deemed possible and practical, even when they disagreed over what exactly that meant.

———

PENNSYLVANIA ABOLITIONISTS never stopped fighting against slavery, and the coalition between black and white reformers in the state grew in a steady trajectory into the 1820s and 1830s. What changed was that white leaders from other areas, many of whom had at least flirted with colonization, began to listen to black Americans and to join the cause for freedom. The movement grew beyond the borders of Pennsylvania, but that does not mean that it languished within the state. We now turn to the shift toward immediate abolition in the North and its effect on the movement in Pennsylvania.

7

THE RISE OF IMMEDIATISM

UCRETIA MOTT WAS AT HOME, probably thinking about the meeting taking place nearby in the Adelphi Building, when her friend Thomas Whitson came to get her on a December morning in 1833. He had been participating in the second day's sessions at the founding convention of the American Anti-Slavery Society (AASS) when it occurred to the men there that the women who shared their passion for the cause of the enslaved might wish to take part in the momentous event. Mott later remembered her shock when Whitson came to her door to invite the women assembled in her kitchen to join the meetings "as spectators or as listeners." "I knew that we were there by sufferance," she recalled in 1863, as she spoke at the American Anti-Slavery Society's Third Decade Convention in Philadelphia. Even so, she; her mother, Anna Folger Coffin; her sister Martha Wright; her daughter Anna Hopper; and her friends Esther Moore, Lydia White, and Sidney Ann Lewis eagerly accepted the invitation.[1]

Looking back on the founding convention from the perspective of the anniversary celebration, Samuel J. May expressed regret that the women had not been invited to sign the group's Declaration of Sentiments. Written and presented at that meeting, the document afterward served as the bedrock of the movement. Mary Grew, a key figure in the Pennsylvania antislavery movement beginning in the late 1830s, asked why the women had not been invited to sign. May admitted that "it would have been thought an impropriety; a thought at which we all laugh now." The omission, he added, "shows that we were in the dark on the subject" and "had no conception of the rights

Lucretia Mott was a crucial figure in Pennsylvania's antislavery movement. (Photo by F. Gutekunst, Philadelphia, PA. Restored by Adam Cuerden. This image is available from U.S. Library of Congress, Manuscript Division. Accessed through Wikimedia Commons.)

of women." Mott harbored no resentment. She may not have signed the document, but neither had she sat by as a spectator. Instead, she had spoken up to offer advice on the wording, and her suggestions had been taken with respect. She explained that "women little knew their influence, or the proper exercise of their own rights."[2]

Undaunted by their lack of experience, abolitionist women in Philadelphia gathered just days after the AASS founding to form their own group, the Philadelphia Female Anti-Slavery Society (PFASS). According to Mott, "there was not a woman capable of taking the chair, and organizing that meeting in due order," so they turned to James McCrummell, a local dentist and leader in the black community, to "give us aid in the work." Mott added that, despite any progress that had been made in the intervening thirty years, "even to the present day, negroes, idiots and women [are] in legal documents classed together; so that we were very glad to get one of our own class to come and aid us in forming that Society." While this comment drew laughter from the audience, it served as a sobering reminder of how much work remained to be done. Even so, by the time of this 1863 gathering, women had learned how to conduct their own meetings. They had also taken leadership roles not only in the PFASS but also in the Pennsylvania Anti-Slavery Society (PASS). A generation after Mott's pioneering work, women like Mary Grew and Sarah Pugh dominated eastern Pennsylvania's antislavery movement.[3]

When the nation's abolitionists met during the Civil War to look back on their achievements and assess their next moves, they had a long history to trace. Both the 1833 and the 1863 conventions included a mixture of women and men, blacks and whites, but by the time the 1863 group met, the climate had changed, not just in the United States but in the antislavery community itself. Women and black Americans had convinced most of their white male allies to think in new ways and to broaden the range of acceptable antislavery tactics. Some historians have maintained that the 1833 convention ushered in major changes to the abolition movement, pitting the earlier generation of "gradualists" against a new generation of "immediatists," but this was not the case. Instead, the 1833 convention offered new energy and opened new doors that allowed the movement to evolve through a series of changes. There was no overnight metamorphosis, and abolitionists would never unify over one particular strategy for ending slavery, but after 1833 more people were empowered to join the movement.

A Broader Movement with More Allies

After the 1833 convention, the Pennsylvania Abolition Society (PAS) continued, as it had for decades, to push freedom beyond the commonwealth's borders and to fight for people "unlawfully held in bondage." It also maintained its agenda of racial uplift and equality by working with black leaders to help freedpersons carve for themselves a place in Pennsylvania society.[4] PAS members persisted in their work toward the first goal until slavery ended, pushing ever onward for an immediate end to human bondage but accepting concessions where they could gain them. The PAS still works toward achieving the second goal, even today, into the twenty-first century. Some PAS members also joined newer groups that emerged, while others remained only in the PAS but worked in close cooperation with the newcomers. Regardless of which affiliations they chose, Pennsylvania abolitionists struggled to define their movement and identify the best tactics for ending slavery. Almost all of them would say that they advocated "immediatism," but few of them could agree on what exactly that meant.

The "immediate" abolition movement grew from several antecedents that can be traced to the early movement. The first, pacifism, came from Quaker doctrine. Mott played a large role in bringing the concept of "pacifism" forward in the post-1833 movement by mentoring William Lloyd Garrison, a New England man who became for many peers and historians the face of antebellum antislavery. Mott and her husband, James, created an important bridge between the PAS and new converts known as "immediatists." They were Hicksite Quakers who believed in traditional Quaker values such as avoiding violence at all costs. This ideology has been a key concept in civil rights efforts throughout the world. Once Mott introduced Garrison to pacifism, he took it further and developed a concept of "nonresistance," which held that all human government, church or state, immorally rested on force.[5]

In addition to passivism, the Motts helped introduce the concept of "free produce" into the new groups. Many activist Quakers before the Motts, including Benjamin Lay, John Woolman, Anthony Benezet, and Warner Mifflin, had refused to use goods produced by enslaved labor. The movement gained attention after English Quaker Elizabeth Heyrick published a pamphlet in 1824 called "Immediate, Not Gradual Abolition," making a case that abolitionists could speed up the end of slavery by boycotting slave-produced goods. Her work gained the attention of Quaker Elias Hicks, and he and his supporters, including the Motts, joined the boycott. James Mott, a merchant who had been dealing in cotton goods, converted his business to deal in wool in 1829. Two years before that, he and several PAS members participated in a meeting in Philadelphia that led to the formation of the Free Produce Society, a group that would elect him as president. Under Lucretia Mott's guidance, the women soon formed an association to buy free produce cotton yarn and spin it into cloth. After that, several free produce stores opened in the city. Black leaders Richard Allen, Robert Purvis, and James Cornish founded the Colored Free Produce Society in 1830, with the Colored Female Free Produce Society soon to follow.[6]

Benjamin Lundy also became heavily involved in the free produce movement and served as a bridge between pre- and post-1833 abolition. He was most influential in taking free produce beyond Quaker abolition and into the larger abolition community. A traveling antislavery lecturer who gained a following in the border South, he eventually ended up in Baltimore, where he opened a free produce store and founded the *Genius of Universal Emancipation*, an antislavery newspaper. Lundy, like most of his generation, remained flexible and willing to employ multiple tactics to secure black freedom, including resettlement or colonization. He sometimes tied resettlement to free produce, hoping that resettled communities would someday grow cotton to compete with that produced by enslaved workers. He appealed to reason and conscience, remaining certain that the way to end slavery would be to convince slaveholders in the South to free their captives voluntarily. By bringing free produce to the forefront and making slavery a moral issue, Lundy, who would move his newspaper to Philadelphia not long after the

AASS founding convention, transformed the antislavery movement, providing a bridge between gradualism and immediatism.[7]

The final factor leading to the AASS convention was the precedent set by black leaders in inaugurating a series of conventions beginning in 1830. The racial climate of the nation had worsened in the 1820s, culminating in a series of racially motivated attacks in Cincinnati, Ohio, in August of 1829. This action was part of a general effort throughout the new states of the Northwest to exclude free blacks from the territory in the interest of maintaining "racial purity." Slavery had been barred from this part of the country by the Northwest Ordinance of 1787, and the new states that were carved out of this territory, most notably Illinois, Indiana, and Ohio, sought to exclude free blacks as well by using anti-immigration legislation to prevent them from settling in their borders. They used Black Laws, or Black Codes, to establish racial control over those who did move in. When those failed, vigilante whites prowled the streets and terrorized black residents. Free blacks from across the North decided to come together to discuss this turn of events and consider whether emigration was the only solution.[8]

The first black convention met at Mother Bethel Church in 1830, and black Americans continued to meet in these conventions every year from 1830 to 1835 and then sporadically until the late 1800s. They would continue to debate various emigration schemes but, overall, their purpose was to determine how they might better their conditions as free blacks in the northern United States. The group supported creating a settlement in upper Canada, but it denounced the American Colonization Society's (ACS) efforts to resettle blacks in Africa. In addition, they discussed education and moral reform. They gained the patronage of white reformers such as the wealthy abolitionist Arthur Tappan, who, along with Benjamin Lundy, S. S. Jocelyn, and William Lloyd Garrison, attended the first convention and discussed the need for a national antislavery society based on the principle of immediate emancipation.[9]

The black conventions set the stage for the interracial change in the antislavery movement that accompanied the founding of the AASS. Black and white leaders had been working together for generations but in a parallel system that was segregated. Black men of the Richard Allen and James Forten generation worked with white allies, but they did not join the PAS. Indeed, Forten's son-in-law Robert Purvis would become the first black man to join the PAS, and he would not do so until 1842. Interaction at the black conventions brought black and white reformers into close contact in an atmosphere of equality, and James Forten built on that momentum to forge a relationship with William Lloyd Garrison. While many white abolitionists tried to walk a fine line and challenge slavery without imperiling the Union or insulting the indifferent, Garrison began pushing unhesitatingly for immediate freedom and full racial equality.[10]

In Philadelphia, Garrison met some of Lundy's Quaker abolitionist friends, who received him warmly and arranged for him to lecture at the Franklin Institute. There he introduced his doctrine of immediate emancipation and blasted colonization as a false reform. His audience included many Quakers, including the Motts, and black leaders, including James Forten. He developed friendships with Lucretia Mott, who coached him on his speaking techniques and discussed antislavery tactics with him, and Forten, who offered him guidance in his crusade against colonization and provided him much-needed financial backing to begin a newspaper of his own, which would call forcefully and unequivocally for uncompensated, immediate abolition, without removal.[11]

Forten also contributed pieces for Garrison's paper, the *Liberator*. He attacked colonization relentlessly, denounced slavery forcefully, and described in detail the racial prejudice that haunted free blacks like himself on a daily basis. He offered Garrison and his readers a firsthand look into black America and helped them understand slavery and abolition in a way that few whites had before. He cited his own service in the Revolutionary War to claim America as his home, and he argued that blacks were tax-paying assets to the community, that the number of black criminals and paupers was smaller than many whites believed, and that blacks took care of their own through mutual aid organizations. His reports illustrate how black-sponsored societies provided a privately operated poor relief system in Philadelphia that made it unnecessary for poor blacks to depend on white tax dollars for support. Forten was one of Garrison's most loyal correspondents, and he provided much of the material Garrison would draw on to write his most famous work, *Thoughts on African Colonization*. That pamphlet and the *Liberator* brought many others into the movement, as black men like Carlisle barber John Peck shared these writings with white reformers like James Miller McKim to expose them to new ideas.[12] By sharing such print materials far and wide, those who opposed both slavery and colonization built a grassroots movement that crossed gender and racial lines.

The 1833 AASS founding convention brought many members of this coalition together in one place for the first time. When PAS leadership learned of plans for the convention, their official response was caution. They were not convinced of "the propriety & wisdom of that movement, *at this particular juncture*," especially in light of "the present tumultuous and distracted state of the political mind" and the frenzy their "brethren of the South" were in. They also suggested it would be unwise to hold a national convention on the principles of immediate emancipation before that term had been clearly defined among the abolition community. The poet John Greenleaf Whittier, a Quaker who would soon move to Philadelphia, used his influence to convince other Quakers to join the meeting and, despite the organizational rejection of the new movement, several PAS members participated. The largest delegation was Philadelphia's group of twelve, making up almost a third of the total participating. Other Pennsylvania delegates came from Chester County, Pittsburgh, Lancaster County, Wilkes-Barre, Allegheny City, and Carlisle. Hostility to the convention was clear from the moment delegates began arriving in the city. Much of the ill feeling was directed toward Garrison and his radical ideas like nonresistance, and many local abolitionists wanted to keep their distance from the reputation he had already acquired.[13]

Three days after the AASS founding convention, a small group of women from Pennsylvania, most of whom were Philadelphia Quakers, formed a female antislavery society based on the same principles as the AASS. The racially integrated group was led by Lucretia Mott and included Pittsburgh's Jane Grey Swisshelm and Philadelphia's Anna Dickinson, Lydia White, Sarah McCrummell, Sidney Ann Lewis, and Grace and Sarah Mapps Douglass, among others. James Forten's wife, Charlotte, and daughters Margaretta, Sarah Louise, and Harriett were there as well. The group met monthly, often in the PAS's Clarkson Hall, and they undertook three main tasks—raising money to cover abolition endeavors such as newspapers and traveling lecturers, visiting and helping black schools, and petitioning Congress. They opened their own school for black children in 1834. In 1836, they began hosting a yearly fair in which they sold fancy goods just before Christmas. These goods contained antislavery slogans and were often made of free produce materials, and the fairs funded most of the AASS and PASS activity. The PFASS outlived all other women's antislavery groups in the United States, disbanding in 1870.[14]

PFASS influence extended well beyond the borders of Pennsylvania. It became one of the strongest abolition societies in the United States, not only funding the male-dominated societies but also spawning a short-lived though influential national movement, the Antislavery Convention of American Women. This group first met in 1837 in New York City, and in 1838 and 1839 in Philadelphia. The PFASS and the Women's Convention both played parts in the rise of the U.S. women's movement through their affiliation with Sarah and Angelina Grimke, sisters from a South Carolina slaveholding family who converted to Quakerism and abolition. Angelina joined the PFASS in 1835, and the group supported her in a controversial speaking tour she undertook throughout the North in 1836–1837.[15]

The men of Philadelphia followed the lead of the women in April 1834 by forming their own immediatist group, the Philadelphia Antislavery Society. The group included a number of PAS members and officers, as well as former officers of the American Convention of Abolition Societies. David Paul Brown was chosen president. Given his long PAS and Abolition Convention history, as well as his standing as one of the city's top lawyers, he was the logical choice to lead the new group. The society's constitution called for both gradual and immediate abolition. It began by reiterating the importance of moral persuasion and pledged to continue PAS efforts to reconstruct Pennsylvania society through racial uplift. It also mentioned plans to urge Congress to ban slavery in the District of Columbia, prevent the admission of additional slave states or territories into the Union, and suppress the internal slave trade. The group concluded by unequivocally stating their goal as "the entire abolition of slavery in the United States, without expatriation," the same goal as the AASS. They maintained that "a large majority of the supporters of the colonization policy" operated by sincere motives, and they were confident that upon "a more full investigation of the subject" they could be brought to "act with us, in promoting the cause of universal freedom."[16]

As evidenced by the number of people active in both the PAS and the new group, the line between "gradual" and "immediate" was blurred. The new societies were meant not to replace the PAS but to reinvigorate the movement. These Philadelphia abolitionists hoped to reach out to southerners, colonizationists, and anyone else they could win over to the cause. Benjamin Lundy and David Paul Brown took the lead in creating this hybrid form of Pennsylvania immediatism. Lundy moved to Philadelphia and started a new antislavery newspaper, the *National Enquirer and General Register*, in 1836. Uninterested in dogmatic debates, he set out to awaken the public to the "*alarming crisis*" slavery posed to the nation and to call attention to "the principles of aggression and marauding violence" that were "spreading over the land." He focused on issues such as free speech and stopping the spread of slavery, issues on which all antislavery advocates could agree.[17]

Lundy and Brown both preferred united action rather than squabbling over differences. Brown presented a definition of "immediate abolition" that fit well with Pennsylvania's antislavery legacy, taking "immediate" to mean that the process of freedom should begin right away, even if the end result took time. He saw the work of the new group as a continuation of PAS efforts. Still optimistic that slaveholders could eventually be brought to reason, he suggested a system of apprenticeship or compensated emancipation, and though he had dismissed the ACS, he suggested a "national colony" where the U.S. government could send free slaves, which was ironically exactly what many ACS founders had hoped to create with Liberia. Borrowing from the PAS, he suggested educating those who remained in slavery in preparation for freedom to take away the "chief argument" against emancipation, and he called for state laws that prohibited manumission to be repealed. Finally, he proposed a national emancipation that replicated Pennsylvania's and asserted the right of abolitionists to speak out against slavery. He also called on his fellow reformers to stop arguing among themselves and antagonizing southerners and colonizationists.[18]

Finally, in 1837 the AASS managed to convince Pennsylvania abolitionists to establish a state society. Lundy used the *National Enquirer* to issue the call for a convention, which met in Harrisburg in 1837. About 250 delegates attended. They discussed a number of issues, including the right of northern states to provide trial by jury to blacks accused of being runaway slaves, the need to protest Texas's admission to the Union, and the role of churches in the abolition movement. Other topics addressed included the internal slave trade, kidnapping of free blacks, free produce, and the importance of women to the movement. They also discussed the need to bring more working-class people into the cause. The group's final act was to make provisions for two executive committees, one for the eastern part of the state and one for the western. The western branch affiliated with the Western Anti-Slavery Society in Ohio within a few years, and the eastern, which drew most of its support from Philadelphia and adjacent counties, took the name Pennsylvania Anti-Slavery Society.[19]

Anti-Abolition and the Politics of Slavery

Even with the relatively mild arguments presented at the convention, the founding of the Pennsylvania Anti-Slavery Society (PASS) caused quite a stir. Within weeks, meetings were held in several parts of the state to denounce abolition, and a new newspaper, the *Anti-Abolitionist*, popped up in Philadelphia. Some anti-abolitionists began calling themselves "Friends of the Integrity of the Union" and planning their own Harrisburg convention.[20] Throughout the early nineteenth century, the central part of the state remained largely hostile to abolition in part due to economic and cultural ties to slave-holding Maryland. In Philadelphia, anti-abolition had been growing alongside the new antislavery movement, and it went hand-in-hand with increased antiblack sentiment. In 1831, after an enslaved man named Nat Turner led an insurrection in Virginia, a group of Philadelphia men met to profess their support for colonization. None of the men listed in the report of the meeting were actual members of the Pennsylvania Colonization Society, and their rhetoric was more heated and more in line with the terrorists who chased black Americans out of Ohio in 1829. They resented southern and midwestern states' efforts to expel free blacks because it sent them seeking asylum in states like Pennsylvania that had no exclusionary laws of their own. The solution, they believed, was for Pennsylvania lawmakers to put an end to black migration into the state and to make provisions to remove blacks already in the state.

Rhetoric turned to violence more than once in Philadelphia, giving the city a reputation for mob action. In 1834, a violent outbreak in the city took the life of a black man who dived into the Schuylkill River to escape a mob. That mob damaged the homes of forty black families over three nights of rioting. That August, a gang of about fifty young white men went looking for a fight throughout the city. During their raid they attacked one of James Forten's younger sons, hitting him on the head, but were thwarted by a white man who knew and respected the Fortens, so the child was not injured badly. A couple of days later, a full-blown rampage began as a fight over the right to enjoy the Flying Horses, a popular carousel that both black and white Philadelphians patronized. Rumors that black youth were disrespecting whites and had stolen equipment from a local fire engine company escalated to the point that black and white adolescents decided to meet at the carousel and fight it out. Within hours, both the carousel and the building that housed it were in ruins. The whites associated with the melee began to prowl the streets of black neighborhoods. Over the course of two nights they broke into a number of houses of black residents and destroyed everything. They also vandalized black churches and beat every black person that came into their path, killing an elderly man and injuring many others. By the end of the attack, they had destroyed an estimated four thousand dollars' worth of property. This basic pattern repeated the next summer. There were many reasons for the violence, including race and class tensions, but one of the strongest flash points was the growth of the new abolition movement.[21]

One response offered by abolitionists was to stress the continuities between the PAS and the PASS to assure Pennsylvanians that there was nothing too radical about the new group. In a series of letters to the *National Enquirer*, J. Blanchard, an agent of the new group, explained that the main difference was the name. Though, he pointed out, an "abolition" society was by definition "antislavery," so even that difference did not mean much. Both societies refused to let slaveholders participate, and both relied on petitioning, organizing societies, holding talks, and publishing antislavery documents. In short, "the two Societies are one in NAME, OBJECT, PRINCIPLE and MEASURES."[22]

Even as they tried to explain their new society to outsiders, Pennsylvania immediatists, like others throughout the nation, continued to argue among themselves. Some wanted to take a stronger stance toward churches, which they argued were not doing their share to combat the immoral system of slavery. Others wanted to use political means to fight the system by campaigning for sympathetic politicians, while others wanted to keep abolition separate from politics. Many wanted to avoid being drawn into these secondary debates. As Lundy tried to explain in the *Enquirer*, divisions only hurt the movement: "We protest against all acrimonious controversies among ourselves. *The* ENEMY *is not yet conquered*." Despite his warnings, the infighting over secondary issues continued.[23]

Not long after Lundy issued this warning, reformers were reminded of the dangers the enemy posed. The PAS and PASS were both facing hostility from whites who resented their efforts, and abolitionists were having an increasingly difficult time finding venues in Philadelphia for their lectures. Members of the two groups came together and formed a committee to build a space they could share. The building they envisioned, which they named Pennsylvania Hall, cost about $40,000 to build. As usual, the PFASS took a leading role in raising the funds, but it was a joint effort by all of the city's abolition groups. The elegant facility opened in May of 1838. In the four days it lasted, it was home to the founding meeting of the American Free Produce Association, the second annual Antislavery Convention of American Women, a lyceum lecture, the PASS offices and annual convention, a free produce store, and Lundy's newspaper, which had been renamed the *Pennsylvania Freeman* and was now being edited by John Greenleaf Whittier. Three days after the building opened, a mob burned it to the ground while spectators and firefighters stood by and watched.

When the attack on the outside of the hall began, abolitionists inside were engaged in the ongoing argument over the exact meaning of "immediate" abolition. David Paul Brown had given the opening speech at the building's dedication, reiterating many of the points he had been making since 1834. William Lloyd Garrison, who had traveled from Boston for the grand opening but had not been asked to speak by Pennsylvania Hall managers, rose to challenge Brown's definition of immediate, accusing him of being tepid in his support for abolition. He also used the opportunity to call out

This image shows firefighters putting water on nearby buildings to prevent the fire from spreading while allowing Pennsylvania Hall to burn. This was indicative of the attitude of most Philadelphians. It took a decade for the owners to see any degree of justice, and, even then, they were unable to recuperate their full loss. (Photo courtesy of Library Company of Philadelphia.)

local colonizationists and challenge them to debates. This intensified an already tense situation both within the Pennsylvania abolition movement and outside the hall.[24]

The loss of Pennsylvania Hall was painful for the city's abolitionists, but, at about the same time, the black community suffered an even worse loss: the vote. As the abolitionists collected money and built their hall, state representatives met in a constitutional convention where some tried to bar black immigration into the state. Failing to do that, they focused on disenfranchising black men, who, up to that point, could vote so long as they owned enough property, just like white men. Delegates decided to revise the property restriction on voting to open the vote to more whites, but added the word "white" to the revised constitution, leaving even the wealthiest black men ineligible to vote. Black and white abolitionists of both the PAS and PASS followed the proceedings in horror.

The PAS acted immediately, turning to black community leader Charles Gardner to help them conduct a census of the city's black population. They hoped to use the census to defend the black community by offering "an unprejudiced comparison" of whites and blacks of similar socioeconomic status. The census revealed that black citizens were, on the whole, industrious, hard-working, and well behaved. In the end, however, it did not matter. Despite the efforts of the PAS and black leaders like Gardner and Forten, black Pennsylvanians lost the right to vote in 1838.[25]

The Movement Splits

The tensions within the abolition movement reached the breaking point in 1840, and the AASS fell apart. Though it took a while, the PASS felt the effects by mid-decade, as Garrison's Pennsylvania supporters purged others, particularly those who supported antislavery politics, from the ranks. The national schism grew from several sources of discord. Confusion over the exact meaning of "immediate emancipation" was one factor, but there were also questions over the role of women in the movement and the relationship between antislavery and other reform movements. The "woman question" was what led to the national break, but it was not a factor in Pennsylvania, where women ran the PFASS and had significant roles in the PASS. The source of dissent in Pennsylvania was over the role of politics in the movement.[26]

Beginning in 1839, abolitionists in New York began working to create an antislavery political party, and many Pennsylvania abolitionists became involved in this movement. One was Dr. F. Julius LeMoyne of Washington, Pennsylvania. The most prominent abolitionist in western Pennsylvania, LeMoyne was known for his work on the Underground Railroad in the area and had been chosen as the first president of the PASS in 1837. He became active in local Liberty Party politics, running several times for governor under that ticket. Thomas Earle was the leading force for the Liberty Party in the eastern part of the state, running for vice president in 1840. Earle was known for his pragmatic attitude and willingness to consider a range of options, including colonization, to secure abolition. He led the defense of black voters in the state constitutional convention and served as James Forten's legal counsel. He tried repeatedly between 1840 and 1845 to argue that the choice to engage in politics was an individual one that should not serve as a test for membership in the PASS.[27]

As editor of the *Pennsylvania Freeman*, Whittier tried to keep peace among the ranks. He refused to print articles not related to antislavery, though he himself favored political action and supported antislavery candidates without going so far as to advocate distinct parties. After Whittier retired, McKim became editor of the paper and maintained an inclusive outlook at first, also supporting political action and the third-party idea. By 1845, however, he came to oppose politics. At the PASS convention that year, he managed to push through strong resolutions opposing both the third party and any participation by abolitionists in the political process. He denounced the U.S. Constitution as a proslavery document and disavowed any voting, office holding under it, or swearing allegiance to it. Soon after, he published an editorial in the *Freeman* declaring that those who were unwilling to accept disunionist and antipolitical views should withdraw from the organization. All the while the PAS continued to allow for a range of ideas within its ranks.[28]

By 1848, the Free Soil Party had replaced the Liberty Party. This party was dedicated to preventing the spread of slavery into new territories, and it too had a significant leader from Pennsylvania. Congressman David Wilmont of Towanda introduced a measure during the Mexican War to forbid slavery in any territories gained from that war. He had become convinced that the South's power had grown too strong and was dictating the fate of the entire nation. His proviso passed the House but was stopped in the Senate by a southern bloc. The Free Soil Party emerged in this atmosphere to lead the charge against southern efforts to spread slavery across the nation.[29]

The election of 1848 saw the rise of Pennsylvania's most famous antislavery politician, Thaddeus Stevens. Elected as a Whig, he had a solid antislavery background that included buying freedom for enslaved people and defending fugitives from slavery in the courts. He refused to sign the 1838 state constitution because it took the vote from black men, and he refused to compromise on the issue of slavery in the territories or the return of fugitives. When the Free Soil Party faded, he helped to organize the Republican Party in 1854.[30]

The Underground Railroad and Armed Self-Defense

Along with the growth of political abolition came expansion of the most radical of all antislavery endeavors, the Underground Railroad. During the Missouri Controversy of 1820, Pennsylvania passed "An Act to Protect Free Negroes and to Prevent Kidnapping," which gave county judges power to try fugitive cases and made it a felony to capture an alleged fugitive without a warrant from a judge. This upset slaveholders in neighboring Maryland, so the Pennsylvania legislature adopted a new law to placate them in 1826, which enabled a master to obtain a warrant from any member of the minor judiciary. In 1842, the fugitive issue made it to the U.S. Supreme Court in the case of *Prigg v. Pennsylvania*. The court unanimously declared Pennsylvania's 1826 personal liberty law unconstitutional and voided other northern states' personal liberty laws. This was essentially a question of state versus federal power, with the Supreme Court maintaining that the Fugitive Slave Act of 1793 superseded all state laws. Pennsylvania responded by passing a new personal liberty law in 1847 that conformed to the *Prigg* parameters, making it a crime for any state judge to hear a fugitive case, for a jailer to use a state prison to detain suspected fugitives, or for anyone to capture an alleged fugitive. This basically made null the Fugitive Slave Act of 1793 in Pennsylvania by using state jurisdiction to deny enforcement of the act.[31]

Pennsylvania abolitionists had long been involved in helping people escape bondage, whether they were with the PAS or the PASS. One of the earliest radical activists, Isaac T. Hopper, was a Hicksite Quaker and a member of the PAS Acting Committee. He gained a reputation in the late 1700s and early 1800s for bending the law by helping captives escape. The PAS as a body operated within the law with the help of David Paul Brown and other lawyers to ensure freedom for fugitives who faced slave catchers as well as free people who faced kidnappers. PASS members also assisted slaves in gaining their freedom through legal and extralegal means. On the legal side, the Pennsylvania legislature opened new avenues in 1847 when they removed the provision of the 1780 law that allowed slave owners who traveled to Pennsylvania to keep their slaves there for six months. On the extralegal side, Vigilance Committees emerged throughout the state.[32]

Philadelphia activists created the first Vigilance Committee in the state. The effort began in 1834, when local black activists came together in frustration from seeing slave catchers chase down free blacks along with fugitive slaves. Purvis played a large role in the growth of the movement after participating in a dramatic rescue of four enslaved brothers. He joined efforts with Forten and convened a group of men in 1837 to form the Vigilant Association of Philadelphia. The goal of this group, as well as the Female Vigilant Association that formed soon after, was to help fugitive slaves and free people who had been kidnapped. McCrummell, the black dentist and community leader who had helped establish the PFASS, played a key role in this endeavor. Similar groups existed in other towns in the region, and they created regional networks that operated in tandem with, but more openly than, the Underground Railroad.

Abolitionists in both the PAS and PASS assisted the Vigilance Committee. Its work expanded after a new Fugitive Slave Act passed in 1850. At that point, William Still and McKim worked to funnel people through the PASS office and along to safety. As word spread of the committee's willingness to help fugitives, enslaved people from throughout the South began to seek their assistance in creative ways, including mailing themselves to the antislavery office in Philadelphia. Henry "Box" Brown shipped himself from Virginia, and Lear Green mailed herself from Maryland. Still, who preserved the records of their daring escapes, worked with PAS member Passmore Williamson on another famous case, that of Jane Johnson and her children. Brought into the state in 1855 by John H. Wheeler, the U.S. ambassador to Nicaragua, Johnson managed to get the attention of Still and Williamson, who responded by rescuing the family. Williamson spent three months in prison before county judge William D. "Pig Iron" Kelley exonerated him. Kelley found two rescuers guilty of assault and battery and gave them a week in jail and a ten-dollar fine. Neither Still nor Williamson were convicted.[33]

Abolitionists of different persuasions also worked together outside Philadelphia, where Underground Railroad activity increased in the 1840s and 1850s. Chester, Columbia, York, Gettysburg, and Chambersburg all became important centers of activity because they were closest to the Mason-Dixon Line. Regardless of which group they affiliated with, activists with the Vigilance Committees and the Underground Railroad were the most radical of the nation's antislavery crusaders.[34]

Through the Vigilance Committees and the Underground Railroad, abolitionists aided escaped slaves on their way to liberty, but the initiative began with the fugitive. As historian Jesse Olsavsky has argued, "their 'underground' mobility provided the foundation for abolitionism's 'aboveground' mobilizations." Women played important roles in all aspects of this militant form of abolition—"as public propagandists, as Underground Railroad Operatives, and as runaways." As they engaged more in fugitive aid, black women tended to favor operating through autonomous organizations, beginning to distance themselves from the PFASS in the 1840s. In 1848, Sarah Mapps Douglass led in founding the all-black Women's Association of Philadelphia.[35]

As sectional tensions intensified, the nation came closer to disunion. The 1850s opened with northerners making yet another concession to southerners through the Compromise of 1850 and the amended Fugitive Slave Act that came with it. Replacing the Fugitive Slave Act of 1793, it threatened the security of all northern free blacks by placing the burden of proof with the presumptive slave rather than the person who claimed to own them. It also denied the accused the right to trial by jury and required law enforcement officers and citizens in general to assist in apprehending accused escapees. It also created a bounty system that incentivized guilty rulings by providing more money for each case in which someone was returned to slavery. Realizing the danger to the union if the law was not respected, most northerners, particularly northern capitalists, reluctantly accepted the new law and their role in its execution. Free blacks embraced self-defense, on the one hand, and emigration, on the other.[36]

A black leader from Pittsburgh named Martin R. Delany embodied both responses. When the Fugitive Slave Act of 1850 was first announced, he pointed out that the law was especially dangerous for northern free blacks, because unlike southern free blacks, they usually did not possess documentation of their status. He then declared that should anyone cross the threshold to his home, he would fight back. Finally, he developed an African emigration scheme that was independent of the American Colonization Society.[37]

As self-defense permeated the atmosphere, it sparked several incidents, one of which took place in Christiana, Pennsylvania, when slaveholder Edward Gorsuch traveled from Maryland to Christiana to capture four fugitives and was met with armed resistance. He and his men responded with gunfire and found themselves under attack by black men and women wielding corn cutters and clubs. People on both sides were injured, and Gorsuch was killed. Castner Hanway, a white man from Christiana who was pulled into the fray when he refused to help the slave catchers, was tried for fomenting war against the United States but was ably defended by Thaddeus Stevens. Lucretia Mott and the PFASS made clothing for the prisoners while they waited for trial in prison, and Mott sat in the courtroom in Independence Hall and watched as Judge Kelley, among others, testified and helped to discredit the prosecution's chief witness. Stevens won a not-guilty verdict, and the whole incident served as evidence that blacks could successfully defend themselves.[38]

The situation in Christiana served as a harbinger of things to come. A couple of years later, fighting broke out between antislavery and proslavery settlers in Kansas and set the stage for the most militant turn in the antislavery movement. Soon after that, abolitionist John Brown offered the cause a martyr and helped spark the Civil War with his botched raid on a military arsenal at Harpers Ferry, Virginia. Pennsylvania abolitionists showed mixed reactions. Mott decried the violence, yet she reached out to Brown's wife to offer comfort while she waited for the day of her husband's execution. McKim traveled with Mary Brown to retrieve her husband's body and help her transport it to New York for the funeral.

While Mott and other pacifists remained confident that only moral suasion should be used in the fight against slavery, Delany met with Brown to hear him out. He refused to join the raid, believing that black liberation should be led by a black leader and not a white man, but he had no qualms about armed self-defense and, when it had a chance of succeeding, revolution. As the Civil War drew near, Delany abandoned his quest to create a black-led settlement in Africa and watched closely as events unfolded in the United

States. When war broke out after Abraham Lincoln's election, it began as a defensive effort to save the Union, but, like other astute abolitionists, Delany knew from the beginning that things could change and that the war could be turned into the opportunity they had all been waiting for: a chance to seize freedom for the enslaved and prove the equality of black men.

———

REGARDLESS OF AFFILIATION, Pennsylvania abolitionists had argued for generations that the key to ending slavery was to convince slaveholders to do the right thing and release their human captives. As this quest failed and the South became increasingly aggressive to the point of suppressing free speech, abolitionists became more militant in defending black human beings and, with the firing on Fort Sumter, southern violence led to northern violence. The Civil War opened another door entirely, but by the time the abolitionists met for their 1863 celebration, it remained to be seen what would come of it all.

While Mott and others looked back fondly on the past thirty years, abolitionist Stephen S. Foster warned them all to look forward as much as backward. As he listened to the speeches at the 1863 convention, he began to fear that his fellow activists had become "over-confident in regard to the success of the movement with which we have so long stood identified." President Abraham Lincoln still had not freed the enslaved, and he was allowing people to be arrested in Washington, DC, and returned to slavery. Foster wanted the president to "proclaim emancipation to the slaves, to the men whom God appoints as the true soldiers of this land" and then let them do the work of ending both the war and slavery. "I will do all in my power to swell the ranks of the Union arm, if you will make the war a war for freedom."[39] Pittsburgh's Martin Delany waited eagerly for the chance to do his part to make that happen.

8

THE CIVIL WAR AND
A SECOND RECONSTRUCTION

STEPHEN FOSTER was not the only one willing to do everything in his power to help in a war for freedom. Black Americans had been waiting for this moment since the days of Phebe and Cuff Dix, and by the time Foster spoke at the American Anti-Slavery Society (AASS) convention in 1864, Martin R. Delany had already approached President Abraham Lincoln and offered to follow the Underground Railroad throughout the South, liberating slaves and organizing them in a large-scale uprising against the Confederacy. He had recently written a novel in which a black character made basically the same trek southward to lead the enslaved people in a rebellion, and the outbreak of the Civil War provided him a chance to make that fantasy a reality while also helping the Union cause.[1]

In presenting his plans to Lincoln and Secretary of War Edwin Stanton, Delany emphasized that he was offering his assistance rather than asking a favor. He suggested that "an army of blacks, commanded entirely by black officers" could "penetrate through the heart of the South, and make conquests, with the banner of Emancipation unfurled, proclaiming freedom as they go, sustaining and protecting it by arming the emancipated [and] taking them as fresh troops." He told Lincoln that his black-led liberation army would "give confidence to the slaves, and retain them to the Union, stop foreign intervention, and speedily bring the war to a close." He emphasized what his plan would do for the country when presenting it to Lincoln, but he was most concerned with what it would do for black Americans.[2]

Martin R. Delany in Union uniform. (Illustration by unknown artist, Wikimedia Commons.)

Delany's bold offer and his recruiting efforts earned him the first field officer's commission granted to a black man in U.S. history. In his uniform, Major Martin R. Delany embodied self-liberation. Delany was one of Pennsylvania's leading black abolitionists in the generation after James Forten. Like Forten, he had flirted with emigration, and he even went so far as to explore Africa in the late 1850s, looking for a place to build a colony. He abandoned that scheme, however, soon after the Civil War began.

Self-Liberation through Civil War

Born in Virginia to an enslaved father and a free mother, Delany and his family were forced to flee to Pennsylvania after he was caught reading. Even in a free state, however, they found daily discrimination. Though Delany had shown intellectual capability from an early age, due to the racial climate in his Pennsylvania community of Chambersburg, he was denied equal educational opportunities. He apprenticed with doctors in Pennsylvania and learned enough to gain acceptance into medical school at Harvard University, only to be forced out after one semester due to white students' objections to his presence. He was a respected leader in the black community, yet he lived at a time when many states would have refused to allow him to settle within their borders, and during which he was relegated to the second-class sections of Pennsylvania's public facilities, such as street cars and schools. After the Compromise of 1850, his freedom came into question, even though he had never been owned by another, because the new Fugitive Slave Law made it almost impossible for free blacks to prove that they were not fugitive slaves. The final blow came in 1857, when the Supreme Court declared through the *Dred Scott* decision that blacks, whether enslaved or free, could not enjoy the protection of the Constitution because they were not U.S. citizens. Even so, throughout most of his life Delany allowed himself to indulge in the hope that black uplift might have a chance in America.

Delany's hopes began to wane in the early 1850s. In 1854, he made a pro-emigration speech to black Americans gathered in Cleveland. At that meeting, he spoke in favor of resettlement to Central or South America, but he soon changed his mind and set his sights on Africa, where he advocated for a colony led by free black Americans without interference from whites. He had come to believe that the twin problems of slavery and racism could "never be changed except by legislation," and that it was "the height of folly to expect such express legislation, except by the inevitable force of some irresistible internal political pressure." In 1859, he and Robert Campbell, an associate who had been teaching at the Institute for Colored Youth, traveled to Africa to find a site for a possible colony.[3]

Like other African American intellectuals, Delany had already cited black service in past wars as a claim to citizenship and equality, and when the Civil War produced the opportunity he had been hoping for, he became eager to extend his self-help philosophy to the battlefield. Believing that pressure from abolitionists could influence the goals and outcome of the war, he hoped that black Americans could prove their worth by fighting and earning the privileges of citizenship. He believed that only blacks could make this a successful war for freedom because, he claimed, "the rights of no oppressed people have ever yet been obtained by a voluntary act of justice on the part of the oppressors."[4]

Even though Lincoln was not the "Great Emancipator" mythologized in popular history, or the hero that abolitionists like Foster wanted him to be, a number of policies under his administration gave black Americans hope even before he officially adopted emancipation. Delany told his earliest biographer that he immediately saw potential in the Lincoln administration and had begun considering ways in which blacks could contribute as early as 1861. He decided to stay and fight once Lincoln issued the Emancipation Proclamation. Seeing black leadership as key, he took heart from the U.S. government's recent recognition of the black independent nations of Haiti and Liberia, a turn of events that he believed "was due more to the presence of intelligent black representatives from Liberia at Washington than a thousand whites." He had long argued, "If I have one great political desire more than another it is that the black race manage their own affairs instead of entrusting them to others." Now was the time to seize the opportunity.[5]

The ad hoc emergency emancipation born of wartime exigencies was quite different from the morally prompted abolition reformers had long fought for, but most abolitionists realized that forming a coalition could help them to push the issue further. Committed nonresistants and Quakers expressed reservations about supporting the war, with Lucretia Mott calling it a "tragic error in the march toward justice," but more pragmatic reformers like her son-in-law Edward M. Davis did support the war. Despite Mott's objections, Davis gained a commission as a captain in the Union Army and used his farm, which was adjacent to the Motts' property, to train black soldiers at Camp William Penn. Leaders like Foster and Delany agreed with Davis's efforts, having determined that abolitionists had a unique opportunity, as well as an obligation, to turn the fight to preserve the Union into a fight against slavery. By the late 1850s, the most radical abolitionists had come to advocate revolt as the only way to end slavery, and the war was offering just such an opportunity.[6]

Though exclusionary policies dampened black Americans' initial enthusiasm for the war, minor victories such as the abolition of slavery in Washington, DC, the diplomatic recognition of Haiti and Liberia, and the acceptance of black troops fueled antislavery optimism. After the Emancipation Proclamation was issued and black troops were accepted into the Union Army, leaders like Delany served as recruiters, and blacks from all stations in life offered their skills as laborers, scouts, and spies. All in all, 8,612 black Pennsylvanians served in Union blue. By the end of the war, eleven regiments of the United States Colored Troops had trained in the state at Camp William Penn, the only training camp set up exclusively for black troops.[7]

During the war, black and white abolitionists expanded their efforts for racial uplift beyond Pennsylvania's borders. James Forten's twenty-five-year-old granddaughter Charlotte built on her family legacy of self-help by going to the South to educate the freed. The first black woman hired to teach in the Sea Islands, she designed a curriculum that taught her pupils about African liberators and heroes. Her work set the precedent for the postwar efforts of the Freedmen's Bureau. Delany went south to help protect the freed in labor disputes, and James Miller McKim resigned his position with the PASS in 1862 to enlist in the freedmen's aid cause by helping refugees in the South

Black soldiers trained at Camp William Penn during the Civil War. (Image courtesy of the Library Company of Philadelphia.)

Carolina Sea Islands. So many northern reformers wanted to help in this endeavor that freedmen's aid societies began to pop up in major cities, including Philadelphia. McKim became general secretary of the Philadelphia Port Royal Relief Association in the spring of 1862, and in 1866 he became corresponding secretary of the American Freedmen's Union Commission. He worked with the latter until it disbanded in 1869. Warner Mifflin's grandchildren also contributed to relief efforts in Port Royal.[8]

A Second Chance at Reconstruction

Despite their contributions during the Civil War, black Americans continued to face second-class treatment throughout the North. Before the war ended, white Pennsylvanians began complaining about black migration to the state. During the war, the fugitive issue became a refugee issue, as thousands of enslaved people took the opportunities offered by disruption and fled to southern Pennsylvania. As white Pennsylvanians argued over what to do with the refugees, the Confederate Army invaded and scooped up blacks without regard to their status. This led to disruption and displacement of the region's black communities as longtime black Pennsylvanians were kidnapped during the raids.[9]

Meanwhile, black leaders and their allies pressed on in their fight for equal rights. Black leaders formed the Pennsylvania State Equal Rights League in 1864 to lead the fight to regain the franchise and other citizenship rights for black Pennsylvanians. White abolitionists like McKim also realized their work remained incomplete and that equal rights needed to be achieved for northern as well as southern blacks. One white leader who was particularly concerned with correcting the voting situation was William D. Kelley, the former judge who had released the defendants in the Jane Johnson case in the 1850s. He had joined the Republican Party in 1854 due to his antislavery convictions, giving up his judgeship to run for federal office and winning re-election a record fifteen times to gain the nickname "Father of the House." Like his fellow Pennsylvania radical Thaddeus Stevens, he was, in historian Ira Brown's words, "an ardent defender of Union supremacy, an advocate of vigorous prosecution of the war, and an active supporter of antislavery measures." He was also an influential member of the Union League of Philadelphia and active in their effort to convince the War Department to organize black troops. He served in Congress from 1861 to 1890, where he remained a strong supporter of Radical Reconstruction and civil rights for black Americans.[10]

After the war, Kelley took a strong stand in favor of black voting rights. He insisted that states allow blacks to vote before being allowed to reenter the Union, and he favored provisions to allow black soldiers to vote. He also pushed to restore black voting in the North. In 1868, John Hickman of Chester County introduced a resolution to strike the word "white" from the constitutional requirements for voting and add a literacy test that would apply to both blacks and whites instead. A coalition of anti-abolitionist Republicans and Democrats thwarted this effort.[11]

The fight for civil rights continued beyond the political arena as well. A transportation revolution had begun in the mid-1800s, facilitating greater ease of travel in boats and by road. Trains and stagecoaches provided for long-distance travel, and horse-drawn streetcars aided mobility within cities. Immediately whites moved to assert their authority by excluding black passengers from stagecoaches, steamships, railcars, and streetcars. Activists fought for equal access to these public conveyances beginning as soon as the streetcars became operational in Philadelphia in 1858. The streetcar situation attracted the attention of civil rights activists during the war, when even blacks in the Union uniform were excluded from the cars or forced to ride on the front platforms, where they were exposed to the weather and to danger.

Reformers called a public meeting at Concert Hall in January of 1865 to address the issue. James Mott and McKim attended and helped present the group's grievances to the nineteen streetcar companies. Company executives resisted by turning to public opinion. They conducted a poll of white passengers to learn, unsurprisingly, that they opposed admitting blacks to the cars. The reformers appealed to the mayor and asked him to prevent city police from ejecting black people from the cars, but the mayor refused to help. After that, they turned to the courts, helping individual blacks fight for their right on a case-by-case basis.[12]

Black reformers also played an important role in this struggle. William Still wrote a letter to newspapers in 1859 to protest exclusion from streetcars, and black leaders founded a number of civil rights organizations to assist in taking test cases to court. These included the Colored People's Union League; the Social, Civil, and Statistical Association of Colored People; and the Equal Rights League. Key figures in the Pennsylvania State Equal Rights League, formed in 1864, included Jonathan C. Gibbs and Octavius V. Catto of Philadelphia and Jonathan Jasper Wright of Luzerne County. Wright later became the first black admitted to the Pennsylvania Bar Association and served as an associate justice of the South Carolina Supreme Court after the war. Catto was the principal of the Institute for Colored Youth in Philadelphia. In the end, the battle over streetcar access was solved by legislators. In 1867, the Pennsylvania General Assembly passed a law against streetcar discrimination that forbade railway corporations from excluding black passengers or segregating the cars.[13]

The schools provided another battlefront in the fight against segregation. As in the days of Delany's youth, black students were denied an education or forced into segregated schools throughout the state. White and black reformers worked to integrate the schools as they had the streetcars, with black reformers again taking the lead. As with the streetcars, integration of the schools was ultimately left to the Pennsylvania General Assembly. The state senate tried to end school segregation in 1874, but their effort failed to gain support in the house. The issue was taken back up in 1881 when Elias H. Allen, a black father in Crawford County, tried to register his children in a white grammar school in Meadville. Allen won his case at the same time that James Sill, a state senator from Erie, was pushing for legislation to end school segregation. The governor signed this legislation in the summer of 1881. From that point forward, it was illegal for schools to make any distinction by race or color among pupils seeking admission or attending public schools in the state.[14]

While these local and statewide struggles played out, the federal government moved to ensure civil rights across the country. First came the Thirteenth Amendment, which followed up on the Emancipation Proclamation by abolishing slavery throughout the country in 1865. Soon after came the 1866 Civil Right Act, which was pushed through Congress due mostly to Thaddeus Stevens's efforts. Kelley also played a role in supporting this act, which declared that all persons born in the United States were citizens, regardless of their race. Two years later this idea was enshrined in the Constitution through the Fourteenth Amendment, which Kelley supported but criticized because it failed to provide for black suffrage. This shortfall was addressed in 1869, when Congress passed the Fifteenth Amendment, which did secure black voting rights across the nation. Finally, the Civil Rights Act of 1875 provided for equal treatment in public accommodations and public transportation, though it did not include education. It was nullified in 1883 when the U.S. Supreme Court ruled that Congress had no jurisdiction over private corporations and thus could not enforce the public accommodations aspects.[15]

Pennsylvania reformers, regardless of how they felt about war, responded with enthusiasm to each of these steps toward reconstructing society in both the North and the South. After the Fifteenth Amendment passed, black Philadelphians held a celebration that included church services, parades down Broad Street, a mass meeting at Horticultural Hall, and a ceremony at the Union League Club that featured an address by Octavius Catto. Robert Purvis and Lucretia Mott, who was almost eighty years old at that point, attended the meeting. Despite the air of optimism, shots fired at some attendees as they returned home after the festivities reminded everyone of the challenges and ill will that remained. That year several thousand black people appeared at the polls in Philadelphia to vote. Though they faced resistance from white Democrats and Republicans alike, they managed to vote due to the intervention of the U.S. Marshal for the Eastern District of Pennsylvania. The next year saw tragedy when a lack of federal troops allowed violence to escalate and led to the murder of three blacks, including Catto.[16]

The PASS continued its work throughout much of this time, disbanding in 1871 when the Fifteenth Amendment was ratified. At that point, the group interpreted its work as being complete, regarding the amendment as the final step in black emancipation. The AASS had dissolved the year before. Realizing that work remained to be done to ensure true equality, the PAS chose to continue fighting. It remains active in the twenty-first century.[17]

IT TOOK AN ALLIANCE OF BLACK AND WHITE ACTIVISTS to win freedom for enslaved blacks. They acknowledged the wrong of human bondage and inequality and worked together to fix it. Early on, people like Phebe and Cuff

Dix laid the foundation by escaping and claiming their own freedom while highlighting the terrible nature of the system from which they ran. Quakers and other idealists forced whites to confront the moral problem of owning human beings. Free black leaders used their positions to gain the attention of ever-widening networks of white supporters of resettlement and make them understand that this country belonged to the very people whose unpaid labor built it. Zealous whites leveraged their passion and used their privilege to fight against slavery and for equality. Finally, pragmatic leaders remained flexible enough to try a combination of social agitation and political action, calling the nation to account over and over and accepting the victories where they could gain them and pushing ever forward for more progress. Each of these components provided an important piece in the overall patchwork of Pennsylvania's antislavery movement.

EPILOGUE

PENNSYLVANIA HAS LONG BEEN KNOWN as the first state to pass an abolition law. Too often that translates into the idea that it was the first state to end human bondage. That is simply not the case. The gradual abolition law did not stipulate immediate freedom for anyone, and evidence indicates that slaves lived and worked in Pennsylvania until the eve of the Civil War. While Pennsylvania took an early lead in addressing the problem of human bondage, its progress was slow and often inadequate, yet the story remains significant for what it tells us about collective effort and persistence.

Historian Ira Brown pointed out that by the time of the post–Civil War Reconstruction, Pennsylvania had fallen behind New England and much of the Midwest in assuring civil rights for black Americans. He described how state action followed in the wake of federal action in a number of areas, including streetcar desegregation, suffrage, and public accommodation in general, concluding that "the Keystone State was in line with, but not ahead of, the main trend of national development in recognizing the rights of blacks." While the second attempt at Reconstruction in the state was more successful than the first, much remains to be done to achieve racial equality in Pennsylvania, as in the rest of the nation.[1]

Getting to the truth of Pennsylvania's complex story of slavery, antislavery, and racial Reconstruction matters still today. On the one hand, if we are allowed to simply celebrate what is positive about the state, including the early antislavery legislation and what, looking back from today's perspective, appears to be a large reform network, we are then also allowed to overlook the hard work and complexity that went into seeking justice for black Pennsylvanians and to feel a celebratory sense that the problems have been corrected and all is right with the world. On the other hand, historian Gary Nash warns that if we focus on the shortfalls and allow ourselves to buy into the notion that abolitionists were "dreamy, unrealistic, meddling fanatics who threatened to tear apart the fragile new nation," we fall into the dangerous possibility of siding with Deep South congressmen and their arguments for states' rights. This completely ignores the fact that there was indeed a right side and a wrong side to this fight, just as today there remains a right side and a wrong side in debates over current civil rights issues. Focusing on the power of those who were on the wrong side of history during the Early Republic years, historian Nicholas Wood warns, leads us to "undervalue the political influence" of activism that was on the right side of history.[2]

Too much emphasis on the victory of abolition also allows us to conveniently forget the reality of how deeply enslavement was embedded in the state's early success. In describing the efforts of preservationists and community activists to accurately recreate the President's House in Philadelphia, historian Marc Ross mentioned one case in which the present has been forced to confront the past and accept it for all its messiness. As the various groups involved in restoring the landmark came together to negotiate the contours of the project, the media attention and public discussion it generated deepened our understanding of slavery. Thanks to these negotiations, "many people realized for the first time that slavery had existed in the North, and in cities, not just on southern plantations." This led many to want to know what had happened and to talk with each other about the relevance to the present. Ross cites many reports of blacks and whites having these conversations together as they collectively tried to come to an understanding of their shared heritage and the ways it shaped their own lives.[3] It is only through such conversations that we can develop a collective memory that is true to all parties and gives us a basis for accepting the mistakes of the past to build a better future that all can share.

NOTES

Introduction

1. Daina Ramey Berry and Kali Nicole Gross, *A Black Women's History of the United States* (Boston: Beacon Press, 2020), 21. Berry and Gross do not write specifically about Phebe, but they write about others in similar circumstances. See also Daina Ramey Berry, *The Price for Their Pound of Flesh: The Value of the Enslaved, from Womb to Grave, in the Building of a Nation* (Boston: Beacon Press, 2017).

2. Darold D. Wax, "Africans on the Delaware: The Pennsylvania Slave Trade, 1759–1765," *Pennsylvania History* 50, no. 1 (January 1983): 38–49, see 46–47. In *A Black Women's History*, Berry and Gross call upon us to "imagine the spaces and fill in the gaps as best as we can" when trying to understand and appreciate the experiences of women and children like Phebe so that we may give them historical voice (20).

3. Marc Howard Ross, *Slavery in the North: Forgetting History and Recovering Memory* (Philadelphia: University of Pennsylvania Press, 2018), 27–28; Lauren Cullivan, "The Meanings behind the Marks: Scarification and the People of Wa," *African Diaspora ISPs*, Paper 4 (1998), http://digitalcollections.sit.edu/african_diaspora_isp/4, accessed 7 September 2019; Dr. Y, "Scarification: An 'Ancient' African Tattoo Culture," *African Heritage* (blog), 16 September 2015, https://afrolegends.com/2015/09/16/scarification-an-ancient-african-tattoo-culture/, accessed 9 September 2019; Katherine Brooks, "This Is the Last Generation of Scarification in Africa," *HuffPost*, 23 September 2014 (updated 6 December 2017), https://www.huffpost.com/entry/scarification_n_5850882, accessed 10 August 2019.

4. Ross, *Slavery in the North*, 13, 46, 49, 83.

Chapter 1

1. Marc Howard Ross, *Slavery in the North: Forgetting History and Recovering Memory* (Philadelphia: University of Pennsylvania Press, 2018), 5, 12, 64. See also Edward Bap-

tist, *The Half Has Never Been Told* (New York: Basic Books, 2016); Phillip Seitz, *Slavery in Philadelphia: A History of Resistance, Denial and Wealth* (Philadelphia: Phillip Seitz, 2014).

2. Edgar J. McManus, *Black Bondage in the North* (Syracuse, NY: Syracuse University Press, 1973), 25–27; Darold Wax, "Negro Imports into Pennsylvania, 1720–1766," *Pennsylvania History* 32, no. 3 (July 1965): 254–287; Darold Wax, "Africans on the Delaware: The Pennsylvania Slave Trade, 1759–1765," *Pennsylvania History* 50, no. 1 (January 1983): 41.

3. Arthur Murphy, "Robert Morris: The Bank of North America," *Encyclopedia of Greater Philadelphia*, 31 August 2015, https://philadelphiaencyclopedia.org/archive /bank-of-north-america/robert-morris/; Robert E. Wright, "Thomas Willing (1731–1821): Philadelphia Financier, and Forgotten Founding Father," *Pennsylvania History* 63, no. 4 (Autumn 1996): 525–526, 533; James Gigantino, "Trading in Jersey Souls: New Jersey and the Interstate Slave Trade," *Pennsylvania History* 77, no. 3 (Summer 2010): 281–302; James Gigantino, "Slavery and the Slave Trade," *Encyclopedia of Greater Philadelphia,* https://philadelphiaencyclopedia.org/archive/slavery-and-the-slave-trade/, accessed 18 November 2019.

4. Daina Ramey Berry and Kali Nicole Gross, *A Black Women's History of the United States* (Boston: Beacon Press, 2020), 20–26.

5. Hugh Thomas, *The Slave Trade* (New York: Simon and Schuster, 1997); Basil Davidson, *The African Slave Trade* (1961; repr., New York: Back Bay Books, 1988); Marcus Rediker, *The Slave Ship: A Human History* (New York: Penguin Books, 2008).

6. Graham Russell Gao Hodges, *Root and Branch: African Americans in New York and East Jersey, 1613–1863* (Chapel Hill: University of North Carolina Press, 1999), 7–12; Edward R. Turner, *Slavery in Pennsylvania: A Dissertation* (Baltimore, MD: Lord Baltimore Press, 1911), 1–2. See also Edward R. Turner, *The Negro in Pennsylvania: Slavery—Servitude—Freedom, 1639–1861* (Washington, DC: American Historical Association, 1911).

7. Jean R. Soderlund, *Quakers and Slavery: A Divided Spirit* (1985; repr., Princeton, NJ: Princeton University Press, 2016), 5–7; Gary Nash and Jean R. Soderlund, *Freedom By Degrees: Emancipation in Pennsylvania and Its Aftermath* (New York: Oxford University Press, 1991), 12.

8. "Colonial Americans at Pennsbury," Pennsbury Manor website, http://www.penns burymanor.org/history/colonial-americans-at-pennsbury/, accessed 20 April 2020; Turner, *Slavery in Pennsylvania*, 11–12; McManus, *Black Bondage*, 5; Gary B. Nash, "Slaves and Slaveowners in Colonial Philadelphia," *William and Mary Quarterly* 30, no. 2 (April 1973): 226, 253–254. See also Jean R. Soderlund, "Black Importation and Migration into Southeastern Pennsylvania, 1682–1810," *Proceedings of the American Philosophical Society* 133, no. 2 (June 1989): 144–153; Larry C. Bolin, "Slaveholders and Slaves of Adams County," *Adams County History* 9 (2003): 1–92; Robert E. Wright, "Slaves in Bucks County, Pennsylvania," *Magazine of Early American Datasets (MEAD)*, University of Pennsylvania Scholarly Commons, McNeil Center for Early American Studies, 21 January 2015, 1–26; Richard G. Johnson, "Blacks in Western Berks: 1760–1930," *Historical Review of Berks County* 60 (1995): 179–181; Richard Johnson, "Slaves in Berks County before 1850," *Historical Review of Berks County* 61 (1996): 159–161 and 184–189; Alan Tully, "Patterns of Slaveholding in Colonial Pennsylvania: Chester and Lancaster Counties 1729–1758,"

Journal of Social History 6, no. 3 (Spring 1973): 284–305; and "Servant & Slavery Records," *Chester County Archives*, https://www.chesco.org/1578/Servant-Slavery-Records, accessed 26 February 2021.

9. Turner, *Slavery in Pennsylvania*, 13; Wax, "Africans on the Delaware," 41; John Alosi, *Shadow of Freedom: Slavery in Post-Revolutionary Cumberland County 1780–1810* (Shippensburg, PA: Shippensburg University Press, 2001).

10. Darold Wax, "The Demand for Slave Labor in Colonial Pennsylvania," *Pennsylvania History* 50, no. 1 (October 1967): 331–332. See also James Gigantino, *The Ragged Road to Abolition: Slavery and Freedom in New Jersey, 1775–1865* (Philadelphia: University of Pennsylvania Press, 2016).

11. Nash, "Slaves and Slaveowners in Colonial Philadelphia," 227–228, quote from letter to Penn at 229, 229–230; McManus, *Black Bondage*, 2; Wax, "Demand for Slave Labor," 341–345.

12. Turner, *Slavery in Pennsylvania*, 13–14; Nash, "Slaves and Slaveowners in Colonial Philadelphia," 230–231, 236, 248–250. For a list of slaveholding elite families, see 248.

13. Wax, "Demand for Slave Labor," 342–344.

14. McManus, *Black Bondage*, 4; Seitz, *Slavery in Philadelphia*, 2, 6, 15; Ross, *Slavery in the North*, 79, 194–195; Phillip R. Seitz, "Tales from the Chew Family Papers: The Charity Castle Story," *Pennsylvania Magazine of History and Biography* 132, no. 1 (January 2008): 65–86. Chew was one of the largest slaveholders, but Curtis Grubb, the owner of the Cornwall Furnace in what is now Lebanon County, registered twenty-five enslaved persons with the Lancaster County clerk in 1780. He was likely the largest slaveholder in the state. John Bezis-Selfa, *Forging America: Ironworkers, Adventurers, and Industrious America* (Ithaca, NY: Cornell University Press, 2003), 185.

15. Wax, "Africans on the Delaware," 44.

16. James Gigantino, "Slavery in the Middle States," *Encyclopedia.com*, https://www.encyclopedia.com/humanities/applied-and-social-sciences-magazines/slavery-middle-states-nj-ny-pa, accessed 3 July 2020; Hodges, *Root and Branch*, 7–12, 17; McManus, *Black Bondage*, 2–4; Ross, *Slavery in the North*, 22.

17. Turner, *Slavery in Pennsylvania*, 17, 20, 22, 26–28; McManus, *Black Bondage*, 55.

18. McManus, *Black Bondage*, 62–73. I thank Cory James Young for pointing out the condition of the slaves for a term.

19. McManus, *Black Bondage*, 74–90. For more on the legal codification of slavery, see "PA Legislation Relating to Slavery," *Adams County History* 9 (2003); and Edward R. Turner, "Slavery in Colonial Pennsylvania," *Pennsylvania Magazine of History and Biography* 35, no. 2 (1911): 141–151.

Chapter 2

1. Billy G. Smith and Richard Wojtowicz, "The Precarious Freedom of Blacks in the Mid-Atlantic Region: Excerpts from the Pennsylvania Gazette, 1728–1776," *Pennsylvania Magazine of History and Biography* 113, no. 2 (April 1989): 250–252; Michael V. Kennedy, "The Hidden Economy of Slavery: Commercial and Industrial Hiring in Pennsylvania, New Jersey and Delaware, 1728–1800," *Essays in Economic and Business History* (2003): 121; John Bezis-Selfa, *Forging America: Ironworkers, Adventurers, and the Industrious Rev-*

olution (Ithaca, NY: Cornell University Press, 2004), 119–120; "History of Hopewell," Friends of Hopewell Furnace NHS website, https://www.friendsofhopewellfurn.org/history-of-hopewell/, accessed 15 June 2019.

2. Darold Wax, "The Demand for Slave Labor in Colonial Pennsylvania," *Pennsylvania History* 50, no. 1 (October 1967): 334–335; Marc Howard Ross, *Slavery in the North: Forgetting History and Recovering Memory* (Philadelphia: University of Pennsylvania Press, 2018), 63.

3. Stephanie Grauman Wolf, "Pennsylvania (Founding)," *Encyclopedia of Greater Philadelphia*, https://philadelphiaencyclopedia.org/archive/pennsylvania-founding/; Jean R. Soderlund, "Native Peoples to 1680," *Encyclopedia of Greater Philadelphia*, https://philadelphiaencyclopedia.org/archive/native-peoples-to-1680/; Marie Basile McDaniel, "Immigration and Migration (Colonial Era)," *Encyclopedia of Greater Philadelphia*, https://philadelphiaencyclopedia.org/archive/immigration-and-migration-colonial-era/, all accessed 2 September 2019.

4. Edgar J. McManus, *Black Bondage in the North* (Syracuse, NY: Syracuse University Press, 1973), 40; Darold Wax, "Africans on the Delaware: The Pennsylvania Slave Trade, 1759–1765," *Pennsylvania History* 50, no. 1 (January 1983): 41; Ross, *Slavery in the North*, 62–66, 198; Graham Russell Gao Hodges, *Root and Branch: African Americans in New York and East Jersey, 1613–1863* (Chapel Hill: University of North Carolina Press, 1999), 112–113; W. Thomas Mainwaring, *Abandoned Tracks: The Underground Railroad in Washington County, Pennsylvania* (Notre Dame, IN: Notre Dame University Press, 2018); "Account with the Plantation," MG 19, Baynton, Wharton and Morgan Papers, General Correspondence, 1758–1799, Pennsylvania State Archives. For more on the social control aspect, see Robert K. Fitts, "The Landscapes of Northern Bondage," *Historical Archaeology* 30, no. 2 (1996): 54–73.

5. Daina Ramey Berry and Kali Nicole Gross, *A Black Women's History of the United States* (Boston: Beacon Press, 2020), 34–35, 52; Erica Armstrong Dunbar, *A Fragile Freedom: African American Women and Emancipation in the Antebellum City* (New Haven, CT: Yale University Press, 2008), 12–13.

6. McManus, *Black Bondage*, 42; Wax, "Demand for Slave Labor," 337–340, 345.

7. Kennedy, "Hidden Economy," 116.

8. Ibid., 119.

9. Ibid., 119–121.

10. John Bezis-Selfa, "Slavery and the Disciplining of Free Labor in the Colonial Mid-Atlantic Iron Industry," *Pennsylvania History* 64 (Summer 1997): 272; Kennedy, "Hidden Economy," 115–117; Berry and Gross, *Black Women's History*, 52–53; Cory James Young, "'JIM, (Alias James Boyd;)': Enslaved Migrant Laborers in the American North," *The Activist History Review*, 15 April 2019, https://activisthistory.com/2019/04/15/jim-alias-james-boyd-enslaved-migrant-laborers-in-the-american-north/.

11. Bezis-Selfa, "Slavery and Disciplining," 272, 277.

12. James Gigantino, "Slavery and the Slave Trade," *Encyclopedia of Greater Philadelphia*, https://philadelphiaencyclopedia.org/archive/slavery-and-the-slave-trade/, accessed 2 September 2019.

13. McManus, *Black Bondage*, 126, 131, 108; Smith and Wojtowicz, "Precarious Freedom," 239; Berry and Gross, *Black Women's History*, 60, 62.

14. Smith and Wojtowicz, "Precarious Freedom," 238; McManus, *Black Bondage*, 108; Berry and Gross, *Black Women's History*, 35–36, 55–56.

15. McManus, *Black Bondage*, 120–122; Smith and Wojtowicz, "Precarious Freedom," 239–240.

16. Edward R. Turner, "Slavery in Colonial Pennsylvania," *Pennsylvania Magazine of History and Biography* 35, no. 2 (1911): 148; Edward R. Turner, *The Negro in Pennsylvania: Slavery—Servitude—Freedom 1639–1861* (Washington, DC: American Historical Association, 1911); McManus, *Black Bondage*, 92; Gigantino, "Slavery and the Slave Trade"; Ross, *Slavery in the North*; Phillip Seitz, *Slavery in Philadelphia: A History of Resistance, Denial and Wealth* (Philadelphia: Phillip Seitz, 2014).

17. Oscar R. Williams, "The Regimentation of Blacks on the Urban Frontier in Colonial Albany, New York City and Philadelphia," *Journal of Negro History* 63, no. 4 (October 1978): 330–332.

18. McManus, *Black Bondage*, 91; Gigantino, "Slavery and the Slave Trade"; James Gigantino, *The Ragged Road to Abolition: Slavery and Freedom in New Jersey, 1775–1865* (Philadelphia: University of Pennsylvania Press, 2016); Edward Baptist, *The Half Has Never Been Told* (New York: Basic Books, 2016); Ibram X. Kendi, *Stamped from the Beginning: The Definitive History of Racist Ideas in America* (New York: Bold Type Books, 2016); Kali N. Gross, *Colored Amazons: Crime, Violence, and Black Women in the City of Brotherly Love, 1880–1910* (Durham, NC: Duke University Press, 2006).

19. McManus, *Black Bondage*, 139–159.

20. Bezis-Selfa, *Forging America*, 120.

Chapter 3

1. Darold D. Wax, "Reform and Revolution: The Movement against Slavery and the Slave Trade in Revolutionary Pennsylvania," *Western Pennsylvania Historical Magazine* 57 (1974): 414–415.

2. Wayne J. Eberly, "The Pennsylvania Abolition Society, 1775–1830" (Ph.D. diss., Pennsylvania State University, 1973), 10; Edward R. Turner, *Slavery in Pennsylvania: A Dissertation* (Baltimore, MD: Lord Baltimore Press, 1911), 130.

3. Richard Newman, "Freedom's Grand Lab: Abolition, Race, and Black Freedom Struggles in Recent Pennsylvania Historiography," *Pennsylvania History* 82, no. 3 (Summer 2015): 358–359; Turner, *Slavery in Pennsylvania*, 64.

4. Eberly, "Pennsylvania Abolition Society," 10; Turner, *Slavery in Pennsylvania*, 65–66; Katharine Gerbner, "'We Are against the Traffick of Men-Body': The Germantown Quaker Protest of 1688 and the Origins of American Abolitionism," *PA History* 74, no. 2 (Spring 2007): 149; Patrick M. Erben, "William Penn, German Pietist(?)," in *The Worlds of William Penn*, ed. Andrew R. Murphy and John Smolenski (New Brunswick, NJ: Rutgers University Press, 2018), 190–216.

5. Gerbner, "We Are Against," 149–150.

6. Turner, *Slavery in Pennsylvania*, 13; Gary B. Nash, "Slaves and Slaveowners in Colonial Philadelphia," *William and Mary Quarterly* 30, no. 2 (April 1973): 254–255; Gerbner, "We Are Against," 152.

7. Gerbner, "We Are Against," 159.

8. The Germantown Protest, reprinted in the *Pennsylvania Magazine of History and Biography* 4 (1880): 28–30. See also Beverly C. Tomek, *Colonization and Its Discontents: Emancipation, Emigration, and Antislavery in Antebellum Pennsylvania* (New York: New York University Press, 2011), 20.

9. Ira Brown, "Pennsylvania's Antislavery Pioneers, 1688–1776," *Pennsylvania History* 55, no. 2 (April 1988): 63; *An Exhortation & Caution to Friends Concerning Buying or Keeping of Negroes* (New York, 1693), reprinted in the *Pennsylvania Magazine of History and Biography* 13 (1889): 265–270; Tomek, *Colonization and Its Discontents*, 20–21. See also Michael Goode and John Smolenski, *The Specter of Peace: Rethinking Violence and Power in the Colonial Atlantic* (Leiden, Netherlands: Brill Publishers, 2018).

10. Nicholas P. Wood and Jean R. Soderlund, "'To Friends and All Whom It May Concerne': William Southeby's Rediscovered 1696 Antislavery Protest," *Pennsylvania Magazine of History and Biography* 141, no. 2 (April 2017): 178–180.

11. Wood and Soderlund, "To Friends," 183–185; Gerbner, "We Are Against," 151, 155, 157; Tomek, *Colonization and Its Discontents*, 21.

12. Wood and Soderlund, "To Friends," 186, 188.

13. Brown, "Pennsylvania's Antislavery Pioneers," 64–65; Eberly, "Pennsylvania Abolition Society," 11; Turner, *Slavery in Pennsylvania*, 130, quote at 131; Gary Nash and Jean Soderlund, *Freedom by Degrees: Emancipation in Pennsylvania and Its Aftermath* (New York: Oxford University Press, 1991), 45.

14. Edgar J. McManus, *Black Bondage in the North* (Syracuse, NY: Syracuse University Press, 1973), 126–127, 150.

15. Nash, "Slaves and Slaveowners," 226, 232, 237; Nash and Soderlund, *Freedom by Degrees*, 71; Ira Brown, *Proclaim Liberty!: Antislavery and Civil Rights in Pennsylvania, 1688–1887* (University Park, PA, 2000, self-published manuscript of essays given to me by Ira Brown), 38.

16. Nash and Soderlund, *Freedom by Degrees*, 42, 62; Nash, "Slaves and Slaveowners," 252; Brown, "Pennsylvania's Antislavery Pioneers," 65; Erica Armstrong Dunbar, *A Fragile Freedom: African American Women and Emancipation in the Antebellum City* (New Haven, CT: Yale University Press, 2008), 13, 14.

17. Turner, *Slavery in Pennsylvania*, 132; Brown, "Pennsylvania's Antislavery Pioneers," 65; Roberts Vaux, *Memoirs of the Lives of Benjamin Lay and Ralph Sandiford: Two of the Earliest Public Advocates for the Emancipation of the Enslaved Africans* (Philadelphia: Solomon W. Conrad, 1815).

18. For the most thorough work on Lay, see Marcus Rediker, *The Fearless Benjamin Lay: The Quaker Dwarf Who Became the First Revolutionary Abolitionist* (Boston: Beacon Press, 2017).

19. Turner, *Slavery in Pennsylvania*, 71, 73–74; Brown, "Pennsylvania's Antislavery Pioneers," 67; Eberly, "Pennsylvania Abolition Society," 15; Jean R. Soderlund, *Quakers and Slavery: A Divided Spirit* (Princeton, NJ: Princeton University Press, 1985), 30–31.

20. Nash, "Slaves and Slaveowners," 252; Wax, "Reform and Revolution," 405, 413.

21. See Beverly C. Tomek, *Pennsylvania Hall: A "Legal Lynching" in the Shadow of the Liberty Bell* (New York: Oxford University Press, 2014), 4, 14; Jon R. Kershner, *John Woolman and the Government of Christ: A Colonial Quaker's Vision for the British Atlantic World* (New York: Oxford University Press, 2018); Geoffrey Plank, *John Woolman's Path to the Peaceable Kingdom: A Quaker in the British Empire* (Philadelphia: University of

Pennsylvania Press, 2012); Thomas P. Slaughter, *The Beautiful Soul of John Woolman, Apostle of Abolition* (New York: Hill and Wang, 2008).

Chapter 4

1. Anthony Benezet, *The Complete Antislavery Writings of Anthony Benezet, 1754–1783*, ed. David L. Crosby (Baton Rouge: Louisiana State University Press, 2013), 113, 115.

2. Anthony Benezet, *Some Historical Account of Guinea, Its Situation, Produce, and the General Disposition of Its Inhabitants: With an Inquiry into the Rise and Progress of the Slave Trade, Its Nature, and Lamentable Effects* (London: J. Phillips, 1771), in *Complete Writings*, 119.

3. Ibid., 179.

4. Ibid., 182–183.

5. Benezet, *Complete Writings*, 1, 2; see Maurice Jackson, *Let This Voice Be Heard: Anthony Benezet, Father of Atlantic Abolitionism* (Philadelphia: University of Pennsylvania Press, 2009).

6. Benezet, *Complete Writings*, 6–7, 13; Jackson, *Let This Voice Be Heard*, xii, xiii; Richard Newman, "Freedom's Grand Lab: Abolition, Race, and Black Freedom Struggles in Recent Pennsylvania Historiography," *Pennsylvania History* 82, no. 3 (Summer 2015): 360; Wayne J. Eberly, "The Pennsylvania Abolition Society, 1775–1830" (Ph.D. diss., Pennsylvania State University, 1973), 16–17.

7. Turner, *Slavery in Pennsylvania*, 134; Darold D. Wax, "Reform and Revolution: The Movement against Slavery and the Slave Trade in Revolutionary Pennsylvania," *Western Pennsylvania Historical Magazine* 57 (1974): 407, 412.

8. Ira Brown, "Pennsylvania's Antislavery Pioneers, 1688–1776," *Pennsylvania History* 55, no. 2 (April 1988): 71–72; James V. Lynch, "The Limits of Revolutionary Radicalism: Tom Paine and Slavery," *Pennsylvania Magazine of History and Biography* 123, no. 3 (July 1999): 187–188.

9. Wax, "Reform and Revolution," 416–417; Brown, "Pennsylvania's Antislavery Pioneers," 72–73; Kirsten Sword, "Remembering Dinah Nevil: Strategic Deceptions in Eighteenth Century Antislavery," *Journal of American History* 97, no. 2 (September 2010): 315–343; Gary Nash and Jean Soderlund, *Freedom by Degrees: Emancipation in Pennsylvania and Its Aftermath* (New York: Oxford University Press, 1991), 80; Christopher Densmore, "Seeking Freedom in the Courts: The Work of the Pennsylvania Society for Promoting the Abolition of Slavery, and for the Relief of Free Negroes Unlawfully Held in Bondage, and for Improving the Condition of the African Race, 1775–1865," *Pennsylvania Legacies* (November 2005): 16–19.

10. Edward R. Turner, *Slavery in Pennsylvania: A Dissertation* (Baltimore, MD: Lord Baltimore Press, 1911), 75–76, 135; Jean R. Soderlund, *Quakers and Slavery: A Divided Spirit* (Princeton, NJ: Princeton University Press, 1985), 103; Wax, "Reform and Revolution," 417.

11. Gary B. Nash, *Warner Mifflin: Unflinching Quaker Abolitionist* (Philadelphia: University of Pennsylvania Press, 2017), 51, 53

12. Ibid., 102.

13. Ibid., 105.

14. Ibid., 106–107.

15. Soderlund, *Quakers and Slavery*, 7.

16. Ira Brown, *Proclaim Liberty!: Antislavery and Civil Rights in Pennsylvania, 1688–1887* (University Park, PA, 2000, self-published manuscript of essays given to me by Ira Brown), 418, 438; Wax, "Reform and Revolution," 418, quoting Pennsylvania Archives, 1st ser., 7:79.

17. Turner, *Slavery in Pennsylvania*, 136–137; Brown, *Proclaim Liberty!*, 38–39; Wax, "Reform and Revolution," 420; James Gigantino, *The Ragged Road to Abolition: Slavery and Freedom in New Jersey, 1775–1865* (Philadelphia: University of Pennsylvania Press, 2016), 255.

18. Wax, "Reform and Revolution," 420–421; Arthur Zilversmit, *The First Emancipation: The Abolition of Slavery in the North* (Chicago: University of Chicago Press, 1967), 127–129; Brown, *Proclaim Liberty!*, 39–41.

19. The state supreme court finally ruled against this practice of extending term slavery to offspring in the 1826 case of *Miller v. Dwilling*. Andrew Diemer, "'The Same Power Which Protects the White Man Should Protect the Black': Pennsylvania, Black Citizenship Rights, and Slavery in the 19th Century," *Pennsylvania Legacies* (Fall 2016): 14.

20. James Gigantino, "Trading in Jersey Souls: New Jersey and the Interstate Slave Trade," *Pennsylvania History* 77, no. 3 (Summer 2010): 282, 283; Edward Baptist, *The Half Has Never Been Told* (New York: Basic Books, 2016).

21. Erica Armstrong Dunbar, *Never Caught: The Washingtons' Relentless Pursuit of Their Runaway Slave, Ona Judge* (New York: 37 Ink/Atria Books/Simon and Schuster, 2017); Turner, *Slavery in Pennsylvania*, 137; Marc Howard Ross, *Slavery in the North: Forgetting History and Recovering Memory* (Philadelphia: University of Pennsylvania Press, 2018), 76.

22. Turner, *Slavery in Pennsylvania*, 61–62; Cook to Batchler, 3 April 1808, MG 8, Colonel Edward Cook Papers 1164, Box 48, Pennsylvania State Archives.

23. Eberly, "Pennsylvania Abolition Society," 20–21. For black Americans and the Revolution, see Douglas R. Egerton, *Death or Liberty: African Americans and Revolutionary America* (New York: Oxford University Press, 2011).

24. Turner, *Slavery in Pennsylvania*, 135–136, 153; Nash and Soderlund, *Freedom by Degrees*, xiv–xv; Robert Fogel and Stanley Engerman, "Philanthropy at Bargain Prices: Notes on the Economics of Gradual Emancipation," *Journal of Legal Studies* 3, no. 2 (June 1974): 377–401.

25. Erica Armstrong Dunbar, *A Fragile Freedom: African American Women and Emancipation in the Antebellum City* (New Haven, CT: Yale University Press, 2008), 28.

Chapter 5

1. Anthony Benezet was perhaps the first abolitionist to use the term "manstealer." See Beverly C. Tomek, *Colonization and Its Discontents: Emancipation, Emigration, and Antislavery in Antebellum Pennsylvania* (New York: New York University Press, 2011), 24; Philip S. Foner, "A Plea against Reenslavement," *Pennsylvania History* 39, no. 2 (April 1972): 239–241; Ira Brown, *Proclaim Liberty!: Antislavery and Civil Rights in Pennsylvania, 1688–1887* (University Park, PA, 2000, self-published manuscript of essays given to me by Ira Brown), 41–42.

2. "Cato to Mr. Printer," *Freeman's Journal*, 21 September 1781, reprinted in Foner, "A Plea against Reenslavement," 239–241.

3. Daniel Meaders, "Kidnapping Blacks in Philadelphia: Isaac Hopper's Tales of Oppression," *Journal of Negro History* 80, no. 2 (Spring 1995): 47–65; Richard S. Newman, *The Transformation of American Abolitionism: Fighting Slavery in the Early Republic* (Chapel Hill: University of North Carolina Press, 2002).

4. Carol Faulkner, *Lucretia Mott's Heresy: Abolition and Women's Rights in Nineteenth-Century America* (Philadelphia: University of Pennsylvania Press, 2013), 2; Cory James Young, "From North to Natchez during the Age of Gradual Abolition," *Pennsylvania Magazine of History and Biography* 143, no. 2 (April 2019): 117–139.

5. See Tomek, *Colonization and Its Discontents*, 51–52.

6. The black population increased by 48 percent from 1810 to 1830, just as foreign immigration from Germany and Ireland grew. The resulting increase in job competition among workers left elites concerned about a perceived increase in the number of paupers and criminals. See William F. Lloyd, "The Roots of Fear: A History of Pennsylvania Hall" (Master's thesis, Pennsylvania State University, 1963), 7, 26–33; *African Repository* 1, no. 12 (February 1826): 384, and *African Repository* 2, no. 7 (July 1826), 153; *Philadelphia in 1824; or, a Brief Account of the Various Institutions and Public Objects in this Metropolis: Being a Complete Guide for Strangers, and an Useful Compendium for the Inhabitants* (Philadelphia: H. C. Carey and I. Lea, 1824), 143; American Colonization Society, *Tenth Annual Report* (Way & Gideon: Washington, DC, 1827), 22. See also Leonard Curry, *The Free Black in Urban America, 1800–1850: The Shadow of a Dream* (Chicago: University of Chicago Press, 1981); Billy G. Smith, *The "Lower Sort": Philadelphia's Laboring People, 1750–1800* (Ithaca, NY: Cornell University Press, 1990); Billy G. Smith, ed., *Down and Out in Early America* (State College: Penn State University Press, 2004); Kali N. Gross, *Colored Amazons: Crime, Violence, and Black Women in the City of Brotherly Love, 1880–1910* (Durham, NC: Duke University Press, 2006). For the role of the Haitian Revolution, see Gary Nash, "Reverberations of Haiti in the American North: Black Saint Dominguans in Philadelphia," *Pennsylvania History* 65 (1998): 44–73.

7. Gary B. Nash, *Warner Mifflin: Unflinching Quaker Abolitionist* (Philadelphia: University of Pennsylvania Press, 2017), 98–100; Codicil of the Will of Anthony Benezet, 13 April 1784, Pennsylvania Abolition Society Papers, vol. 1 (1748–1789), 59; Wax, "Reform and Revolution," 424.

8. Wayne J. Eberly, "The Pennsylvania Abolition Society, 1775–1830" (Ph.D. diss., Pennsylvania State University, 1973), 26–27, 54–58; Tomek, *Colonization and Its Discontents*, 28; Pennsylvania Abolition Society, "Manumission Book A, 1780–1793" (AmS 05), 242–243, Historical Society of Pennsylvania; Wax, "Reform and Revolution," 424.

9. Dee E. Andrews, "Reconsidering the First Emancipation: Evidence from the Pennsylvania Abolition Society Correspondence, 1785–1810," *Pennsylvania History* 64 (Summer 1997): 230–249, esp. 236–237; Nash, *Warner Mifflin*, 144.

10. Arthur Zilversmit, *The First Emancipation: The Abolition of Slavery in the North* (Chicago: University of Chicago Press, 1967), 157–158; Stanley I. Kutler, "Pennsylvania Courts, the Abolition Act, and Negro Rights," *Pennsylvania History* 30, no. 1 (January 1963): 14–27; Christopher Densmore, "Seeking Freedom in the Courts: The Work of the Pennsylvania Society for Promoting the Abolition of Slavery, and for the Relief of Free Negroes Unlawfully Held in Bondage, and for Improving the Condition of the African

Race, 1775–1865," *Pennsylvania Legacies* (November 2005): 18; Erica Armstrong Dunbar, *A Fragile Freedom: African American Women and Emancipation in the Antebellum City* (New Haven, CT: Yale University Press, 2008), 2; Kutler, "Pennsylvania Courts," 15–18.

11. Edward R. Turner, *Slavery in Pennsylvania: A Dissertation* (Baltimore, MD: Lord Baltimore Press, 1911), 138–139; Kutler, "Pennsylvania Courts," 26–27.

12. Gary Nash, *Forging Freedom: The Formation of Philadelphia's Black Community, 1720–1840* (Cambridge, MA: Harvard University Press, 1988), 2.

13. Nicholas P. Wood, "A 'Class of Citizens': The Earliest Black Petitioners to Congress and Their Quaker Allies," *William and Mary Quarterly*, 3rd ser., 74, no. 1 (January 2017): 109–144; Nash, *Forging Freedom*; Richard S. Newman, *Freedom's Prophet: Bishop Richard Allen, the AME Church, and the Black Founding Fathers* (New York: New York University Press, 2009); Emma Lapsansky-Werner, "Teamed Up with the PAS: Images of Black Philadelphia," *Pennsylvania Legacies* 5, no. 2 (November 2005): 11–15. See also Andrew Diemer, "Reconstructing Philadelphia: African Americans and Politics in the Post-Civil War North," *Pennsylvania Magazine of History and Biography* (January 2009): 29–58; Andrew Diemer, *The Politics of Black Citizenship: Free African-Americans in the Mid-Atlantic Borderland, 1817–1863* (Athens: University of Georgia Press, 2016).

14. Julie Winch, *A Gentleman of Color: The Life of James Forten* (New York: Oxford University Press, 2003); Janice Sumler-Lewis, "The Forten-Purvis Women of Philadelphia and the American Anti-Slavery Crusade," *Journal of Negro History* 66, no. 4 (Winter 1981–1982): 281–288; Tomek, *Colonization and Its Discontents*, 132–162; Diemer, "Same Power," 14; Philip Lapsansky, "'Abigail, a Negress': The Role and the Legacy of African Americans in the Yellow Fever Epidemic," in *A Melancholy Scene of Devastation: The Public Response to the 1793 Philadelphia Yellow Fever Epidemic*, ed. J. Worth Estes and Billy G. Smith (Sagamore Beach, MA: Watson Publishing International, 1997), 63; Thomas E. Will, "Liberalism, Republicanism, and Philadelphia's Black Elite in the Early Republic: The Social Thought of Absalom Jones and Richard Allen," *Pennsylvania History* 69, no. 4 (Autumn 2002): 560.

15. Tomek, *Colonization and Its Discontents*, 31–34.

16. Andrews, "Reconsidering the First Emancipation," 241; Tomek, *Colonization and Its Discontents*, 136–137.

17. Margaret Hope Bacon, "The Pennsylvania Abolition Society's Mission for Black Education," *Pennsylvania Legacies* (November 2005): 21, 22, https://hsp.org/sites/default/files/imagecache/baconlegaciesarticle.pdf; Tomek, *Colonization and Its Discontents*, 29–30; Wood, "A 'Class of Citizens,'" 135.

18. Eberly, "Pennsylvania Abolition Society," 148–162.

19. Ibid.; Tomek, *Colonization and Its Discontents*, 32.

20. Pennsylvania Abolition Society, Minutes, 19 October 1789, PAS Papers, Historical Society of Pennsylvania; Eberly, "Pennsylvania Abolition Society," 162–163.

21. Tomek, *Colonization and Its Discontents*, 137.

22. J. A. Dunn, "Philadelphia not Philanthropolis: The Limits of Pennsylvania Antislavery in the Age of the Haitian Revolution," *Pennsylvania Magazine of History and Biography* 135, no. 1 (January 2011): 73–102; Larry Tise, *American Counterrevolution: A Retreat from Liberty, 1783–1800* (Mechanicsburg, PA: Stackpole Books, 1998); Gary B. Nash, "Slaves and Slaveowners in Colonial Philadelphia," *William and Mary Quarterly*

30, no. 2 (April 1973): 223–256; Roberts Vaux, "Minutes of the Proceedings of the 12th Annual American Convention of Abolition Societies," 2 October 1827, PAS Papers, Historical Society of Pennsylvania; Tomek, *Colonization and Its Discontents*, 35–36, 137; Robert Proud, "Notes of Memoranda," MG 8, Robert Proud Papers 221, Pennsylvania State Archives.

23. Tomek, *Colonization and Its Discontents*, 137; Will, "Liberalism, Republicanism, and Philadelphia's Black Elite," 567–568.

24. Tomek, *Colonization and Its Discontents*, 53; Le Roy Hopkins, "The Negro Entry Book: A Document of Lancaster County's Antebellum African American Community," *Journal of the Lancaster County Historical Society* 88 (1984): 142–180; Armstrong Dunbar, *Fragile Freedom*, 49.

25. Margaret Hope Bacon, *But One Race: The Life of Robert Purvis* (Albany: State University of New York Press, 2007), 17; Julie Winch, "Philadelphia and the Other Underground Railroad," *Pennsylvania Magazine of History and Biography* 111, no. 1 (January 1987): 3–25; James Forten, *Letters from a Man of Colour, on a Late Bill before the Senate of Pennsylvania* (Philadelphia, 1813); Tomek, *Colonization and Its Discontents*, 138; Densmore, "Seeking Freedom in the Courts," 18.

26. Armstrong Dunbar, *Fragile Freedom*, 44; Daina Ramey Berry and Kali Nicole Gross, *A Black Women's History of the United States* (Boston: Beacon Press, 2020), 56, 67, 68.

27. "200 Years of Black Pennsylvania, Part I, 1776–1900," *New Pittsburgh Courier*, 18 December 1976; Armstrong Dunbar, *Fragile Freedom*, 6.

28. Beverly C. Tomek, *Pennsylvania Hall: A "Legal Lynching" in the Shadow of the Liberty Bell* (New York: Oxford University Press, 2014); Emma J. Lapsansky-Werner, "'Since They Got Those Separate Churches': African Americans and Racism in Jacksonian Philadelphia," in *African Americans in Pennsylvania: Shifting Historical Perspectives*, ed. Joe William Trotter Jr. and Eric Ledell Smith (University Park: Penn State University Press, 1996), 93–120.

29. Tomek, *Colonization and Its Discontents*, 37–39.

30. Beverly C. Tomek, "'From motives of generosity, as well as self-preservation': Thomas Branagan, Colonization, and the Gradual Emancipation Movement," *American Nineteenth Century History* 6, no. 2 (June 2005): 121–147; Tomek, *Colonization and Its Discontents*, 36; James V. Lynch, "The Limits of Revolutionary Radicalism: Tom Paine and Slavery," *Pennsylvania Magazine of History and Biography* 123, no. 3 (July 1999): 195.

31. Letters from Richard Bailey to PAS, 16 August 1820, (AmS 02), Folders 1, 17, PAS Papers (see also Reels 13, 17), File 2, Historical Society of Pennsylvania; Beverly C. Tomek, "Seeking 'An Immutable Pledge from the Slaveholding States': The Pennsylvania Abolition Society and Black Resettlement," *Pennsylvania History* 75, no. 1 (2008): 27–53.

32. Tomek, "Seeking 'An Immutable Pledge'"; Tomek, *Colonization and Its Discontents*.

33. See Richard Archer, *Jim Crow North: The Struggle for Equal Rights in Antebellum New England* (New York: Oxford University Press, 2017).

34. William Wright, *Columbia Spy*, 4 October 1834, quoted in Willis L. Shirk Jr., "Testing the Limits of Tolerance: Blacks and the Social Order in Columbia, Pennsylvania," *Pennsylvania History* 60, no. 1 (January 1993): 35–50.

35. Andrews, "Reconsidering the First Emancipation," 243.

Chapter 6

1. Phillip R. Sietz, "Tales from the Chew Family Papers: The Charity Castle Story," *Pennsylvania Magazine of History and Biography* 132, no. 1 (January 2008): 66–78. Homewood is now a museum: see http://www.museums.jhu.edu/homewood.php.

2. October 1814 Deposition of Roderick Burgess; Charles Carroll of Carrollton to Robert Goodloe Harper, 29 October 1814; Charles Carroll to Benjamin Chew, 8 November 1814; and Dr. Nathaniel Chapman to Benjamin Chew, 29 November 1814, all in Seitz, "Tales from the Chew Family Papers," 72–75.

3. For information on William Lewis, see "A Tour of Abolitionism in Philadelphia," WHYY.org, 9 February 2018, https://whyy.org/segments/a-tour-of-abolitionism-in -philadelphia-3/; "Judge William Lewis," Historic Strawberry Mansion, http://www.his toricstrawberrymansion.org/aboutus/judge-william-lewis/. For the correspondence on the case, see 14 December 1814, Opinion of William Lewis; Benjamin Chew to William Lewis, 14 December 1814; and William Lewis to Benjamin Chew, 16 December 1814, all in Seitz, "Tales," 76–78. See also Edward R. Turner, "The First Abolition Society in the United States," *Pennsylvania Magazine of History and Biography* 36, no. 1 (1912): 92–109, and Benjamin Chew to William Rawle, 16 December 1814, and William Rawle to Benjamin Chew, 19 December 1814, both in Seitz, "Tales," 79–81; William Lewis to Harriet Chew Carroll, 22 December 1814, Harriet Chew Carroll to Benjamin Chew, 23 December 1814, Benjamin Chew (as Harriet) to William Lewis, 24 December 1814, and William Lewis to Mrs. Charles Carroll (Harriet), 24 December 1814, all in Seitz, "Tales," 84–86.

4. Richard Newman, "Freedom's Grand Lab: Abolition, Race, and Black Freedom Struggles in Recent Pennsylvania Historiography," *Pennsylvania History* 82, no. 3 (Summer 2015): 362–363, 368.

5. Dee E. Andrews, "Reconsidering the First Emancipation: Evidence from the Pennsylvania Abolition Society Correspondence, 1785–1810," *Pennsylvania History* 64 (Summer 1997): 235, 236; Stanley Harrold, *Border War: Fighting Over Slavery before the Civil War* (Chapel Hill: University of North Carolina Press, 2010); Richard S. Newman, *The Transformation of American Abolitionism: Fighting Slavery in the Early Republic* (Chapel Hill: University of North Carolina Press, 2002); Nicholas P. Wood, "Considerations of Humanity and Expediency: The Slave Trades and African Colonization in the Early National Antislavery Movement" (Ph.D. diss., University of Virginia, Corcoran Department of History, 2013), iii.

6. Nicholas P. Wood, "A 'Class of Citizens': The Earliest Black Petitioners to Congress and Their Quaker Allies," *William and Mary Quarterly*, 3rd ser., 74, no. 1 (January 2017): 115; Wood, "Considerations of Humanity," 2, 4. See also A. Glenn Crothers, *Quakers Living in the Lion's Mouth: The Society of Friends in Northern Virginia, 1730– 1865* (Gainesville: University Press of Florida, 2012); and James Gigantino, *The Ragged Road to Abolition: Slavery and Freedom in New Jersey, 1775–1865* (Philadelphia: University of Pennsylvania Press, 2016).

7. Wood, "Considerations of Humanity," 3; Gary B. Nash, *Warner Mifflin: Unflinching Quaker Abolitionist* (Philadelphia: University of Pennsylvania Press, 2017), 4, 94.

8. Wood, "A 'Class of Citizens,'" 116–120, 110, 126, 139, 113.

9. Nash, *Warner Mifflin*, 137, 160, 161.

10. Nash, *Warner Mifflin*, 121–123, 139, 146.

11. Wayne J. Eberly, "The Pennsylvania Abolition Society, 1775–1830" (Ph.D. diss., Pennsylvania State University, 1973), 180–193; "Circular of President of PAS," 27 July 1831, and "Reply of New York Society," 15 August 1837, both in PAS Minutes, 1825–1847, PAS Papers, Historical Society of Pennsylvania.

12. Nash, *Warner Mifflin*, 126–128, 189; Wood, "Considerations of Humanity," 5, 7, 17.

13. Edward Baptist, *The Half Has Never Been Told* (New York: Basic Books, 2016); Daina Ramey Berry, *The Price for Their Pound of Flesh: The Value of the Enslaved, from Womb to Grave, in the Building of a Nation* (Boston: Beacon Press, 2017).

14. Christopher Densmore, "Seeking Freedom in the Courts: The Work of the Pennsylvania Society for Promoting the Abolition of Slavery, and for the Relief of Free Negroes Unlawfully Held in Bondage, and for Improving the Condition of the African Race, 1775–1865," *Pennsylvania Legacies* (November 2005): 18; Beverly C. Tomek, *Pennsylvania Hall: A "Legal Lynching" in the Shadow of the Liberty Bell* (New York: Oxford University Press, 2014), 22.

15. Eberly, "Pennsylvania Abolition Society," 67–70.

16. Andrew Diemer, "'The Same Power Which Protects the White Man Should Protect the Black': Pennsylvania, Black Citizenship Rights, and Slavery in the 19th Century," *Pennsylvania Legacies* (Fall 2016): 14–16; Nash, *Warner Mifflin*, 203–204; Densmore, "Seeking Freedom in the Courts," 18.

17. See Lucy Maddox, *The Parker Sisters: A Border Kidnapping* (Philadelphia: Temple University Press, 2016); Richard Bell, *Stolen: Five Free Boys Kidnapped into Slavery and Their Astonishing Odyssey Home* (New York: 37 Ink/Simon and Schuster, 2019).

18. "The Slave Question in Missouri and Arkansas," *Niles Weekly Register*, 6 November 1819; Pennsylvania Antislavery Society, *Twenty-First Annual Report*, 1858, (Philadelphia: Merrihew & Thompson, 1858), 9; Wood, "Considerations of Humanity," 17.

19. Beverly C. Tomek, *Colonization and Its Discontents: Emancipation, Emigration, and Antislavery in Antebellum Pennsylvania* (New York: New York University Press, 2011), 63–92.

20. Tomek, *Colonization and Its Discontents*, 58, 60–61; Tomek, *Pennsylvania Hall*, 23.

21. Wood, "Considerations of Humanity," 355; Ryan P. Jordan, *Slavery and the Meetinghouse: The Quakers and the Abolitionist Dilemma, 1820–1865* (Indianapolis: Indiana University Press, 2007); Paul Buckley, *The Essential Elias Hicks* (San Francisco: Inner Light Books, 2013).

22. Edward Bettle, "Notices of Negro Slavery, As Connected with Pennsylvania," read before the Historical Society of Pennsylvania, 7 August 1826, PAS Papers, Historical Society of Pennsylvania; "Slavery in the District of Columbia," *Niles' Register*, 31 January 1828; Nash, *Warner Mifflin*, 218; Wood, "A 'Class of Citizens,'" 114; Wood, "Considerations of Humanity," 4.

Chapter 7

1. American Anti-Slavery Society, *Proceedings of the American Anti-Slavery Society at Its Third Decade, Held in the City of Philadelphia, December 3rd and 4th, 1864* (New York: American Anti-Slavery Society, 1864), 40–43; *Friends' Intelligencer and Journal*, 1 June

1901, (58), 344; Carol Faulkner, *Lucretia Mott's Heresy: Abolition and Women's Rights in Nineteenth-Century America* (Philadelphia: University of Pennsylvania Press, 2013), 64.

2. American Anti-Slavery Society, *Proceedings of the American Anti-Slavery Society*, 41–42.

3. Ibid., 43. For more on the PFASS and women's involvement in antislavery in general, see Jean Fagan Yellin and John C. Van Horne, eds., *The Abolitionist Sisterhood: Women's Political Culture in Antebellum America* (Ithaca, NY: Cornell University Press, 1994).

4. Beverly C. Tomek, *Colonization and Its Discontents: Emancipation, Emigration, and Antislavery in Antebellum Pennsylvania* (New York: New York University Press, 2011); Paul Polgar, *Standard-Bearers of Equality: America's First Abolition Movement* (Chapel Hill: University of North Carolina Press, 2019).

5. Margaret Hope Bacon, "By Moral Force Alone: The Antislavery Women and Nonresistance," in *Abolitionist Sisterhood*, ed. Jean Fagan Yellin and John C. Van Horne (Ithaca, NY: Cornell University Press, 1994), 276; Beverly C. Tomek, *Pennsylvania Hall: A "Legal Lynching" in the Shadow of the Liberty Bell* (New York: Oxford University Press, 2014), 29, 54; William Whipper, "Address on Non-Resistance to Offensive Aggression," *The Colored American*, 9 September 1837.

6. Carol Faulkner, "The Root of the Evil: Free Produce and Radical Antislavery, 1820–1860," *Journal of the Early Republic* 27 (Fall 2007): 377–405; Wendell Phillips Garrison, "Free Produce among the Quakers," *Atlantic Monthly* 22, no. 132 (October 1868): 485–494; Norman B. Wilkinson, "The Philadelphia Free Produce Attack upon Slavery," *Pennsylvania Magazine of History and Biography* 66 (July 1942): 294–313. See also Margaret Hope Bacon, "Lucretia Mott: Pioneer for Peace," *Quaker History* 82 (Fall 1993): 63–79; and Faulkner, *Lucretia Mott's Heresy*. For a good overview of the free produce movement, see Julie Holcomb, *Moral Commerce: Quakers and the Trans-Atlantic Boycott of the Slave Labor Economy* (Ithaca, NY: Cornell University Press, 2016).

7. Tomek, *Pennsylvania Hall*, 15–16.

8. Stephen Middleton, *The Black Laws: Race and the Legal Process in Early Ohio* (Athens: Ohio University Press, 2005); Howard H. Bell, *Minutes of the Proceedings of the National Negro Conventions, 1830–1864* (New York: Ayers Publishing, 1969).

9. Richard S. Newman, *Freedom's Prophet: Bishop Richard Allen, the AME Church, and the Black Founding Fathers* (New York: New York University Press, 2009), 268–269; Philip S. Foner, *History of Black Americans: From the Emergence of the Cotton Kingdom to the Eve of the Compromise of 1850* (New York: Greenwood Press, 1983); Lucien Holness, "National Negro Convention Movement," *Encyclopedia of Greater Philadelphia*, https:// philadelphiaencyclopedia.org/archive/national-negro-convention-movement/, accessed 15 May 2019.

10. David Walker, *Walker's Appeal in Four Articles: Together with a Preamble, to the Coloured Citizens of the World*, 3rd ed. (Boston, 1830); Tomek, *Pennsylvania Hall*, 27–29.

11. Tomek, *Pennsylvania Hall*, 29; Asa Earl Martin, "Pioneer Anti-Slavery Press," *Mississippi Valley Historical Review* 2, no. 4 (March 1916): 509–528; Julie Winch, *A Gentleman of Color: The Life of James Forten* (New York: Oxford University Press, 2003), 241.

12. Tomek, *Colonization and Its Discontents*, 132–162; American Anti-Slavery Society, *Proceedings of the American Anti-Slavery Society*, 32–33.

13. Edwin P. Atlee, D. Mandeville, Thomas Shipley, and George Griscom to Arthur Tappan and other Abolitionists of New York, 7 October 1833, PAS Papers, Historical

Society of Pennsylvania; Ira Brown, *Proclaim Liberty!: Antislavery and Civil Rights in Pennsylvania, 1688–1887* (University Park, PA, 2000, self-published manuscript of essays given to me by Ira Brown), 78–79, 82, 87, 93–94, 139; Anna Davis Hallowell, *James and Lucretia Mott, Life and Letters, edited by their Granddaughter* (Boston: Houghton Mifflin and Company, 1884), 112, 115; John Greenleaf Whittier, "The Antislavery Convention of 1833," *Atlantic Monthly* 33 (February 1874): 166–172, esp. 166.

14. Brown, *Proclaim Liberty!*, 166; Richard Newman, "Freedom's Grand Lab: Abolition, Race, and Black Freedom Struggles in Recent Pennsylvania Historiography," *Pennsylvania History* 82, no. 3 (Summer 2015): 32; Philip Lapsansky, *We Abolition Women Are TURNING THE WORLD UPSIDE DOWN!*, exhibition catalog for an exhibit commemorating the 150th anniversary of the Antislavery Convention of American Women, 1837, 1838, 1839, Library Company of Philadelphia, March–June, 1989, 6; Faulkner, *Lucretia Mott's Heresy*, 66; Ira Brown, *Mary Grew: Abolitionist and Feminist, 1813–1896* (Selingsgrove, PA: Susquehanna University Press, 1996); Ashley Council, "Ringing Liberty's Bell: African American Women, Gender, and the Underground Railroad," *Pennsylvania History* 87, no. 3 (Summer 2020): 494–531.

15. Kathryn Kish Sklar, *Women's Rights Emerges within the Antislavery Movement: 1830–1870, A Brief History with Documents* (Boston: Bedford/St. Martin's, 2000); Tomek, *Pennsylvania Hall*, 48–53; Faulkner, *Lucretia Mott's Heresy*, 72.

16. *Constitution of the Philadelphia Antislavery Society.* Instituted Fourth Month, 30th, 1834 (Philadelphia: Thomas Town, Walnut Street, 1834); David Paul Brown, *An Oration, Delivered, By Request, Before the Antislavery Society of New York, on the Fourth of July, 1834* (Philadelphia: T. K. Collins, 1834), 3; *First Annual Report of the Board of Managers of the Philadelphia Antislavery Society: Read and Accepted at the Annual Meeting of the Society, July 4th, 1835* (Philadelphia: Printed By Order of the Society, 1835).

17. *National Enquirer*, 3 August 1836.

18. Brown, *Oration*, 10, 12, 18, 20–29.

19. Brown, *Proclaim Liberty!*, 117, 142, 143–145; Pennsylvania Antislavery Society, *Proceedings of the Pennsylvania Convention, Assembled to Organize a State Antislavery Society, at Harrisburg, on the 31st of January and 1st, 2nd, and 3rd of February* (Philadelphia: Merrihew and Gunn, 1837), 7; "Abolition," *Free At Last? Slavery in Pittsburgh in the 18th and 19th Centuries*, University of Pittsburgh, http://exhibit.library.pitt.edu/freeatlast/abolition.html, accessed 20 May 2019.

20. "Pro-Slavery Convention in Pennsylvania!!!," *National Enquirer*, 25 February 1837; "The Friends of the Integrity of Union," *National Enquirer*, 22 April 1837; "Anti-Abolitionist," *National Enquirer*, 15 July 1838; Beverly C. Tomek, "The Economization of Freedom: Abolitionists versus Merchants in the Culture War That Destroyed Pennsylvania Hall," *Canadian Review of American Studies* 47, no. 2 (Summer 2017), 171–198.

21. Henry Mayer, *All On Fire: William Lloyd Garrison and the Abolition of Slavery* (New York: W. W. Norton, 2008), 189; Tomek, *Pennsylvania Hall*, 36–39; Beverly Wilson Palmer, *Selected Letters of Lucretia Coffin Mott* (Urbana: University of Illinois Press, 2002), 29; "The Tyranny of Prejudice," *National Enquirer*, 24 February 1837.

22. "Our Principles," *National Enquirer*, 4 March 1837, 18 March 1837; "Address from the Antislavery Convention to the Citizens of Pennsylvania," reprinted in the *National Enquirer*, 25 March and 1 April 1837; "A Quaker" (reprinted from the *Delaware County Republican*), *National Enquirer*, 20 July 1837.

23. "J. Blanchard's Speech," *National Enquirer,* 20 May 1837; "General Assembly," *National Enquirer,* 17 July 1837; "More Sound Doctrine," *National Enquirer,* 5 October 1837; "The Time for Action," *National Enquirer,* 5 October 1837; "Controversies among Abolitionists," *National Enquirer,* 12 October 1837; "Awake Thou That Sleepest!," *National Enquirer,* 12 April 1838; "Clerical Sensitiveness," *National Enquirer,* 12 April 1838; Lewis G. Gunn, "General Assembly," *National Enquirer,* 8 July 1837. For Lundy's quote, see "Party Politics," *National Enquirer,* 28 January 1837.

24. Tomek, *Pennsylvania Hall,* 45–62.

25. Pennsylvania Abolition Society, *To the Present State and Condition of the Free People of Color, of the City of Philadelphia* (January 1838), 3–7, available from the Library of Congress, https://www.loc.gov/resource/rbaapc.22520/?sp=35, accessed 28 February 2021.

26. Brown, *Proclaim Liberty!,* 146–147, 231.

27. Polgar, *Standard-Bearers of Equality,* 292; Brown, *Proclaim Liberty!,* 234–244.

28. Brown, *Proclaim Liberty!,* 246–249, 250–256.

29. Ibid., 270–274.

30. David G. Smith, *On the Edge of Freedom: The Fugitive Slave Issue in South Central Pennsylvania, 1820–1870* (New York: Fordham University Press, 2013).

31. Brown, *Proclaim Liberty!,* 275–276.

32. Christopher Densmore, "Seeking Freedom in the Courts: The Work of the Pennsylvania Society for Promoting the Abolition of Slavery, and for the Relief of Free Negroes Unlawfully Held in Bondage, and for Improving the Condition of the African Race, 1775–1865," *Pennsylvania Legacies* (November 2005): 19; Daniel Meaders, "Kidnapping Blacks in Philadelphia," *Journal of Negro History* 80, no. 2 (Spring 1995): 47–65; Daniel Meaders, *Isaac Hopper's Tales of Kidnapping and Oppression in Philadelphia 1780–1843* (Cherry Hill, NJ: Africana Homestead Legacy Publishers, 2009); Mrs. George A. Dayton, "The Underground Railroad and Its Stations in Bradford County," *The Settler, A Quarterly Magazine of History and Biography,* Bradford County Historical Society, April 1953, 142–148, in MG 142, John R. Haudenshield Papers, MG 143, Sarah R. Meseroll Collection, and MG 180, Millicent Barton Rex Collection, Pennsylvania State Archives; "The Slave Case," *Friend: A Religious and Literary Journal,* 4 November 1848.

33. Beverly C. Tomek, "Vigilance Committees," *Encyclopedia of Greater Philadelphia,* https://philadelphiaencyclopedia.org/archive/vigilance-committees/; Brown, *Proclaim Liberty!,* 283–284; Daina Ramey Berry and Kali Nicole Gross, *A Black Women's History of the United States* (Boston: Beacon Press, 2020), 77–78.

34. W. Thomas Mainwaring, *Abandoned Tracks: The Underground Railroad in Washington County, Pennsylvania* (Notre Dame, IN: University of Notre Dame Press, 2018); Smith, *On the Edge of Freedom.* See also Richard Blackett, *The Captive's Quest for Freedom: Fugitive Slaves, the 1850 Fugitive Slave Law, and the Politics of Slavery* (New York: Cambridge University Press, 2018).

35. Jesse Olsavsky, "Women, Vigilance Committees, and the Rise of Militant Abolitionism, 1835–1859," *Slavery and Abolition* 39, no. 2 (2018): 357–382; Jesse Olsavsky, "Runaway Slaves, Vigilance Committees, and the Pedagogy of Revolutionary Abolitionism," in *A Global History of Runaways: Workers, Mobility, and Capitalism, 1600–1850,* ed. Marcus Rediker, Titus Chakraborty, and Matthias van Rossum (Oakland: University of California Press, 2019), 216–233, quote at 214; Erica Armstrong Dunbar, *A Fragile Free-*

dom: African American Women and Emancipation in the Antebellum City (New Haven, CT: Yale University Press, 2008), 69–71, 94–95.

36. Stanley W. Campbell, *The Slave Catchers: Enforcement of the Fugitive Slave Law, 1850–1860* (New York: W. W. Norton, 1970); Andrew Diemer, "'The Same Power Which Protects the White Man Should Protect the Black': Pennsylvania, Black Citizenship Rights, and Slavery in the 19th Century," *Pennsylvania Legacies* (Fall 2016): 17; Carol Wilson, "'Active Vigilance Is the Price of Liberty': Black Self-Defense against Fugitive Slave Recapture and Kidnapping of Free Blacks," in *Antislavery Violence: Sectional, Racial, and Cultural Conflict in Antebellum America*, ed. John R. McKivigan and Stanley Harrold (Knoxville: University of Tennessee Press, 1999), 108–127.

37. Tomek, *Colonization and Its Discontents*, chap. 7; Robert S. Levine, *Martin R. Delany: A Documentary Reader* (Chapel Hill: University of North Carolina Press, 2003).

38. James Kopaczewski, "Christiana Riot Trial," *Encyclopedia of Greater Philadelphia*, https://philadelphiaencyclopedia.org/archive/christiana-riot-trial/, accessed 15 July 2020; Thomas P. Slaughter, *Bloody Dawn: The Christiana Riot and Racial Violence in the North* (New York: Oxford University Press, 1991).

39. American Anti-Slavery Society, *Proceedings of the American Anti-Slavery Society*, 59.

Chapter 8

1. J.W.C. Pennington to Editor, *Weekly Anglo-African*, 15 April 1865, describing a 28 March 1865 speech by Delany; Frank A. Rollin, *Life and Public Services of Martin R. Delany* (Boston: Lee and Shepard, 1883), 159–160, 185.

2. Rollin, *Life and Services*, 158, 162, 166, 168–169; Delany to Stanton, 15 December 1863, in *The Black Abolitionist Papers*, Vol. 5, *The United States, 1859–1865*, ed. C. Peter Ripley (Chapel Hill: University of North Carolina Press, 1992), 261–264.

3. R.J.M. Blackett, "Return to the Motherland: Robert Campbell, A Jamaican in Early Colonial Lagos," *Phylon* 40, no. 4 (1979): 375–386.

4. Delany, "Political Destiny," in Rollins, *Life and Services*, 355.

5. Rollins, *Life and Services*, 137, 39–40, 128–129; Victor Ullman, *Martin R. Delany: The Beginnings of Black Nationalism* (Boston: Beacon Press, 1971), 263, 268, 278; Robert S. Levine, *Martin Delany, Frederick Douglass, and the Politics of Representative Identity* (Chapel Hill: University of North Carolina Press, 1997), 189; William Wells Brown, *The Rising Son; or, the Antecedents and Advancement of the Colored Race* (Boston: A.G. Brown, 1874), 348; Delany to Douglass, *Douglass' Monthly*, September 1862.

6. Donald Yacovone, ed., *A Voice of Thunder: A Black Soldier's Civil War* (Urbana: University of Illinois Press, 1999), 26–33; James McPherson, *The Negro's Civil War: How American Negroes Felt and Acted during the War for the Union* (New York: Pantheon Books, 1965), 11; Henry Highland Garnet, "An Address to the Slaves of the United States of America (Rejected by the National Convention, Held in Buffalo, N.Y., 1843)," reprinted in Sterling Stuckey, *The Ideological Origins of Black Nationalism* (Boston: Beacon Press, 1972), 165–173; George Lawrence Jr., in the *Weekly Anglo-African*, 13 April and 27 April, 1861, reprinted in Ripley, *Black Abolitionist Papers*, 5:110–112; Margaret Hope Bacon, "Lucretia Mott: Pioneer for Peace," *Quaker History* 82 (Fall 1993): 63–79, quote at 74.

7. Yacovone, *Voice of Thunder*, 26–57; Donald Scott Sr. and Donald Scott Jr., *Camp William Penn (Images of America: Pennsylvania)* (Mount Pleasant, SC: Arcadia Publish-

ing, 2008); Mark Lardas, *African American Soldier in the American Civil War: USCT 1862–66* (New York: Osprey Publishing, 2006).

8. Janice Sumler-Lewis, "The Forten-Purvis Women of Philadelphia and the American Anti-Slavery Crusade," *Journal of Negro History* 66, no. 4 (Winter 1981–1982): 285; Ira Brown, *Proclaim Liberty!: Antislavery and Civil Rights in Pennsylvania, 1688–1887* (University Park, PA, 2000, self-published manuscript of essays given to me by Ira Brown), 153–155; Daina Ramey Berry and Kali Nicole Gross, *A Black Women's History of the United States* (Boston: Beacon Press, 2020), 95.

9. John M. Broomal to Maurice Makenroe, 19 December 1866, in MG 8, John M. Broomal Papers 33; Michael Schall Jr. to Michael Schall Sr., 11 February 1831, and John Bachman to J. J. Bierer, 12 February 1862, both in MG 253, Jacob J. Bierer Papers, Pennsylvania State Archives; Andrew Diemer, "'The Same Power Which Protects the White Man Should Protect the Black': Pennsylvania, Black Citizenship Rights, and Slavery in the 19th Century," *Pennsylvania Legacies* (Fall 2016): 18; Brown, *Proclaim Liberty!*, 154; David G. Smith, *On the Edge of Freedom: The Fugitive Slave Issue in South Central Pennsylvania, 1820–1870* (New York: Fordham University Press, 2013), 173, 181–185.

10. Brown, *Proclaim Liberty!*, 336–338, 339.

11. Ibid., 340–346, 367–369, 351; *Congressional Globe*, 38th Congress, 2nd Session, 16 January 1865, 287.

12. Elizabeth Stordeur Pryor, *Colored Travelers: Mobility and the Fight for Citizenship before the Civil War* (Chapel Hill: University of North Carolina Press, 2016), 45; Brown, *Proclaim Liberty!*, 363–366; *Report of the Committee Appointed for the Purpose of Securing to Colored People in Philadelphia the Right to the Use of Streetcars* (Philadelphia, 1867), Historical Society of Pennsylvania.

13. Brown, *Proclaim Liberty!*, 364, 366–368; Richard Newman, "Freedom's Grand Lab: Abolition, Race, and Black Freedom Struggles in Recent Pennsylvania Historiography," *Pennsylvania History* 82, no. 3 (Summer 2015): 368. For Catto's full story, see Daniel R. Biddle and Murray Dubin, *Tasting Freedom: Octavius Catto and the Battle for Equality in Civil War America* (Philadelphia: Temple University Press, 2010), esp. 345–351; Memorial by Colored Peoples' Union League Association of Philadelphia to Senate and House of Representatives of Pennsylvania, 14 January 1865, in MG 15, 1865, Pennsylvania State Archives.

14. Brown, *Proclaim Liberty!*, 362–363, 373. See also Hugh Davis, *"We Will Be Satisfied With Nothing Less": The African American Struggle for Equal Rights in the North during Reconstruction* (Ithaca, NY: Cornell University Press, 2011).

15. Brown, *Proclaim Liberty!*, 351–352, 347, 369–370. See also John T. Cumbler, *From Abolition to Rights for All: The Making of a Reform Community in the Nineteenth Century* (Philadelphia: University of Pennsylvania Press, 2008).

16. Biddle and Dubin, *Tasting Freedom*, 421–473.

17. Brown, *Proclaim Liberty!*, 369–371.

Epilogue

1. Ira Brown, *Proclaim Liberty!: Antislavery and Civil Rights in Pennsylvania, 1688–1887* (University Park, PA, 2000, self-published manuscript of essays given to me by Ira Brown), 375.

2. Gary B. Nash, *Warner Mifflin: Unflinching Quaker Abolitionist* (Philadelphia: University of Pennsylvania Press, 2017), 12–13; Nicholas P. Wood, "A 'Class of Citizens': The Earliest Black Petitioners to Congress and Their Quaker Allies," *William and Mary Quarterly*, 3rd ser., 74, no. 1 (January 2017): 113.

3. Marc Howard Ross, *Slavery in the North: Forgetting History and Recovering Memory* (Philadelphia: University of Pennsylvania Press, 2018), 140–142, 176, 251–253.

INDEX

Beverly C. Tomek is Associate Professor of History and Associate Provost for Curriculum and Student Achievement at the University of Houston–Victoria. She is the author of *Colonization and Its Discontents: Emancipation, Emigration, and Antislavery in Antebellum Pennsylvania* and *Pennsylvania Hall: A "Legal Lynching" in the Shadow of the Liberty Bell*, as well as the coeditor of *New Directions in the Study of African American Recolonization*.